MW01017084

"Singaporeans love ghost stories. Singapore's most popular book series is not Harry Potter but the infernally successful collection of *True Singapore Ghost Stories*. And why not? We in Southeast Asia are blessed with possibly the most imaginatively gruesome horror culture in the world."

— Colin Goh in *The Sunday Times*

"Think Singapore bestseller, and thoughts will inevitably turn to a volume of *True Singapore Ghost Stories*."

— *The Straits Times*

Angsana Books

The Almost Complete Collection Of

True Singapore Ghost Stories

BOOK 13

Russell Lee
& team of ghost writers

Angsana Books

Published by  Angsana Books

Angsana Books is an imprint of

FLAME OF THE FOREST PUBLISHING Pte Ltd
Blk 5 Ang Mo Kio Industrial Park 2A
#07-22/23, AMK Tech II, Singapore 567760
Tel: (65) 6484 8887, Fax: (65) 6484 2208
mail@flameoftheforest.com

FLAME OF THE FOREST PUBLISHING
95085 North Bank Rogue Road A/B
Gold Beach, Oregon 97444-9543 USA
Tel: (541) 247 2924, Fax: (541) 247 0373
info@flameoftheforest.com

www.flameoftheforest.com

Cover by Mangosteen Designs

Printed in Singapore

ISBN 981-3056-98-3

For SJG,
Wisdom be yours

My hands don't earn me too much gold,
For security when I grow old,
But we'll all be equal under the grass,
And God's got a heaven for Country Trash.

—*Country Trash*,
by Johnny Cash

AUTHOR'S NOTE

After Book 12 was completed late last year, I made a huge effort to meet as many readers as I possibly could. I went to schools, did bookshop signings and even managed some storytelling sessions at the Robinsons Christmas Village. But one of the most rewarding experiences that I've had was the storytelling session at a children's home in Sembawang. I was literally moved to tears. The kids refused to let me leave after I had been with them for a while and told them some tales that I thought were heartwarming. The event was organised by the thoughtful National Association of Travel Agents of Singapore. Do let me know if you wish me to visit any group of children. I'd be thrilled to be of service.

The students of Holy Innocents' Primary School went to so much trouble to say thank you with their lovely self-made cards and imaginative cut-outs. A picture of the array of cards is on the back inside cover.

I did not meet fans. I met friends. For that's how much these encounters mean to me. Sure, I wasn't able to share as much time as I wanted to but in the little time that I had, I did try my best to spread as much cheer and goodwill as I could, especially during the Christmas period when Book 12 was launched. I hope you liked the end-of-the-year gifts I handed out.

In this book, stories by readers feature prominently once again. I do "clean up" and make them the best that they can be. I try to retain the unique flavour of every story though. The story matters much more to me than the way the story is told.

I have tried to ensure that each story is indeed true. As far as I can tell, the story-tellers are all serious about their encounters with the supernatural.

I hope you'll like the stories by Maia Lee, the swinging Singapore Idol singer who's just released a new album. She's not only a rising star but also a very nice person who has strong views on just about every subject you talk to her about. Maia has "the third eye". She's featured in The Russell Lee Interview. I also met

Russell Lee meets the feisty Maia Lee.

child actress Winona Wee of CHIJ (Kellock) Primary School. Their stories are a fun read.

My team of writers is growing and the latest to join is Becs. She's 16 going on 17 and loves all things black, and songs by Simple Plan and Good Charlotte. She's afraid of flying though.

The *True Singapore Ghost Stories* series is selling steadily and the sales have exceeded 700,000 copies. Please do make very sure that the book you buy has the ANGSANA mark. There are many who are trying to cash in by publishing ghost stories but you know you have the real thing in your hands when you see the Angsana mark on the *True Singapore Ghost Stories* book you buy.

Enjoy this book and do write me. I look forward to hearing from you and reading your stories. If your story is chosen for publication, you'll win cash and other prizes!

Cheers.

russelllee@flameoftheforest.com

Dear Readers,

Thanks for all your letters and stories. A special hello to Connie Yamada. I hope you are feeling much better these days. Take care of yourself.

Please do not be discouraged if your story is not selected. Try until it is. Don't give up easily.

I've been receiving numerous email. Please do use email if that's your preference. You can reach me at this address: russelllee@flameoftheforest.com.

Congratulations to all those who did very well in The Angsana Russell Lee Writers' Contest (Book 12).

The winners:

ALVIN TAY ZHI YUAN
Blk 9, Teck Whye Lane
AMY CHIANG
Blk 206A Compassvale Lane
BRENDA LEE XIAO TIAN
Blk 107 Towner Rd
CHARLENE WONG
6th floor, Bangunan Hj. Ahmad
Laksamana b.Othman, Jln Sultan,
Bandar Seri Begawan
DERICK NG GEM PENG
Blk 127 Bedok North St 2
ERIC TAN CHEE HOW
Relau Indah Condo, Persiaran Bt
Jambul 1, Pulau Pinang

EVIE TAN WEI WEI
Persiaran Bt Jambul 1, Relau Indah
Condo, Pulau Pinang
GLORIA KAVITHA
Blk 694 Hougang St 61
IVY TAN
Blk 814 Tampines St 81
JOSEPH LEE WEN WEI
Blk 521 Woodlands Dr
MARION LEE
Singapore
NATASHA ISMAIL
Blk 253A Ang Mo Kio St 21

ONG ANN HUAT IAN
Blk 603 Ang Mo Kio Ave 5
POLIN ANAK GUMBEK
Blk AR-02-06, Subang GoodYear
Count 10, Subang Jaya, Selangor
PRISCILLA CHEW
5 Tua Kong Green
RAIHAN BTE IBRAHIM
Blk 39 Bedok South Rd
RONRICH TAN
Blk 662C Jurong West St 64
YONG FUNG LAN
Api-Api Centre, Blk 1, 2nd Floor,
Kota Kinabalu, Sabah

And thanks for your letters:

ADRIAN TAN
Blk 864 Jurong West St 81
AMANDA HO SOK YEE
Blk 335A, Smith St
AMARLINA
Singapore
ANDRE
Singapore
ANDREW MAH SHI JIE
Blk 511 Pasir Ris St 52
ANDY YO WEI QIANG
Blk 533 Serangoon North Ave 4
ANG WAN TING
Blk 207 Petir Rd
ANG YIN JIE
Blk 662 Jln Damai
ANIS SARAGIH
Singapore
ANNABEL WOO YING JIE
Blk 540 Jurong West Ave 1

ANNABELLE LIM SZE MIN
Blk 893C Woodlands Dr 50
ANONYMOUS
Blk 142 Bt Panjang Petir Rd
ANONYMOUS
Blk 55 Toa Payoh Lor 5
ARINI BINTE MOHD ADINAN
Blk 704 West Coast Rd
ATHRAJ
Blk 527 Choa Chu Kang St 51
AW WAN YEE
Tmn Jubilee, Phase III, Lengkok
Niaph, Penang
AZEEM ARAFAT BIN MOHD RAZIFF
Blk 568 Choa Chu Kang St 52
B.BAVANI
Blk 119B Kim tian Rd
BAI ANNI
Blk 28, Telok Blangah Dr
BASIL FRANCIS RODRIGUES
Blk 217 Ang Mo Kio Ave 1

BENJAMIN CHENG YUMENG
Blk 28 Toa Payoh Lor 6
BOH CHIT PANG
Blk 181 Jelebu Rd
BRENDAN POH
Blk 101 Bt Purmei Rd
BRIAN WAN
USJ 1612B UEP Subang Jaya
CALEAN CHIA YULING
31 Springside Link
CALEB ANG
Blk 288E Bt Batok St 25
CARLISSIA KEW HUI MIN
Blk 651A Jurong West St 61
CHAMMON NG
27 Jln Puteh Jerneh
CHAN KA SHING
Blk 101A Toa Payoh Lor 2
CHAN TSIN YI
Jln Parit Mahang 26/28, Taman Bt
Saga, Shah Alam, Selangor

CHARMAGNE BUTCHER
  Blk 408 Sin Ming Garden
CHARMAINE YE SHUN MEI
  Blk 294 Choa Chu Kang Ave 2
CHEN WENYI
  Blk 535 Ang Mo Kio Ave 5
CHEN XIN JUAN
  Blk 107 Yishun Ring Rd
CHENG YU BOON
  Blk 102 Bedok North Ave 4
CHNG YEOH BENG
  Green Rd One, Penang
CHOW POI YEE
  8 Boon Lay Dr, Summerdale
CHRISTABEL CHAI
  Blk 164 Bishan St 13
CHRISTINA CHE YONG CHUN
  Blk 531 Serangoon North Ave 4
CHUA KAI YANG
  Blk 12 North Bridge Rd
CHUA SOON HUI
  Blk 664A Jurong West St 64
CHUA YI LING
  Blk 98 Whampoa Dr
CHYNNA ANG
  46 Gardenia Rd
DANNY WONG
  Lrg Kempas 6A1, Everbright Jaya,
  Jln Kemaps, Kuching, Sarawak
DARREN CHONG SHUN HAO
  Blk 343 Tampines St 33
DARREN CHUA
  Blk 106 Bt Purmei Rd
DARREN NGO
  Blk 507 Choa Chu Kang St 51
DARREN THNG
  Blk 498B Tampines St 43
DASMOND
  Blk 303 Canberra Rd
DEEPAN SEKERAN
  Blk 899A Woodlands Dr 50
DENNIS LIM
  Blk 522 Jurong West St 52
DEREK TAN DING WEI
  Blk 226 Tampnes St 23
DERICK NG GEM PENG
  Blk 127 Bedok North St 2
DIANA BTE M. ITHNIN
  Blk 738 Woodlands Circle
DIANA TAN KWEE SUAN
  Blk 589B Montreal Dr
DIANATHA CHONG WEI PING
  Blk 128A PunggolField Wallk
EDEN MAKILAN
  2 Chung Park
EDWINA LIM
  53 Westwood Ave
EILEEN GOH YULING
  Blk 115 Rivervale Walk
EMERLINE
  84 Jln Chempaka Kuning
EMILY HO
  Singapore
ERNEST FOO
  3 Oxford Rd Kentish Lodge
ESTHER TAN
  Blk 291D Bt Batok St 24
EUGENE LAU
  Blk 8 Simei St 1 Melville Park
EVANGELINE CHAI
  Blk 164 Bishan St 13
FARANABILAH BTE JEMAHAT
  Blk 456 Choa Chu Kang Ave 4
FLORINE LO HUI SHAN
  Blk 207B Compassvale Lane

FOO JIE YI
  Blk 246 Hougang St 22
FOONG WAI LING
  Blk 542 Choa Chu Kang St 52
GALVIN YIP KAH HOE
  Blk 24 Beo Crescent
GEORGINA
  Blk 44 Owen Rd
GOH CHUI LING
  1 Amber Rd Amber Point
GOH JIA MIN
  Blk 718 Hougang Ave 2
GOH JOEK SENG
  Blk 108 Ang Mo Kio Ave 4
GOH KIA YEOW
  27 Lorong Lew Lian
GRACE GOH
  Jln 2, Taman Sri Ukay, Ampang
  Selangor
GUI MIN
  Jln Mutiara, Mutiara View
HALIJA MOSAH
  503B Canberra Link
HARVIN
  Jln Teratai 44, Taman Johor Jaya, JB
HO XING LIN KIN
  Blk 899A Woodlands Dr 50
HO YENG HAO
  Blk 765 Pasir Ris St 71
HUN MING KWANG
  Blk 115 Bedok North Rd
IAN AMIRUL BIN KAMEL
  Blk 408 Yishun Ave 6
IFRAN SHAMAL BIN SAMSUDIN
  Blk 133 Pasir Ris St 11
JACQUELINE
  Blk 44 Owen Rd
JADELINE TAY BI HUI
  Blk 129 Bt Batok Ave 6
JASMINE ANG
  Blk 81A Toa Payoh Lor 4
JESSICA TEO
  Blk 127 Rivervale St
JESSIE DAS
  Blk 402 Sin Ming Ave
JETH HO YONG JU
  Blk 544 Serangoon North Ave 3
JOEY TOH
  Blk 266 Bishan St 24
JOHN TAY
  Blk 103 Jln Rajah
JOHNSON F. XAVIER
  Utara 5 Taman Desa Pinji, Lahat,
  Perak
JONATHAN YEO
  Blk 135 Edgefield Plains
JOSELINE CHUA XIN MAN
  Blk 546 Bedok North St 3
KEE TZE PHENG
  Persiaran Bekor 4, Taman Buluh
  Emas, Ipoh
KELLY NEO
  Blk 238 Serangoon Ave 2
KELVIN CHANG HOCK CHAI
  Blk 113 Bedok North St 2
KENNY MOSES
  Tabuan Jaya Polis Komplek, Jln Setia
  Raja, Kuching, Sarawak
KHO MIN HAO ALEXANDER
  Blk 259 Ang Mo Kio Ave 2
KOH CHEN YEE
  10 Stirling Rd, Queens Condominium
KOH LUO HAO
  Blk 73 Geylang Bahru
KOH WEN JIE
  Singapore

KOK ZHI MING
  Ang Mo Kio Ave 6
KRISTEN MOSES
  Tabun Jaya Police Complexs, Jln Setia
  Raja, Kuching, Sarawak
LAI CUI FENG
  Blk 421 Pasir Ris Dr 6
LEON NEO
  Blk 147 Mei Ling St
LIANA
  Singapore
LIANG YU LIN
  Blk 660 Woodlands Ring Rd
LIM JIA YAN
  40 Loyang View
LIM MING HUI
  Blk 545 Serangoon North Ave 3
LIM SHAO HAN
  Blk 113 Teck Whye Lane
LIM WEI SHENG
  Blk 19 Teck Whye Lane
LIM ZHI HUI
  Blk 395 Bt Batok West Ave 5
LINDA CHAN SHIA WAH
  Blk 7-8-25, Ltg Paya Terubong 3, Air
  Itam, Pulau Pinang
LOK SHUEN-LI
  Blk 633, Hougang Ave 8
LOW LIEW PUAY
  Blk 22 Sin Ming Rd
LYON KOH YUAN QUAN
  Blk 213 Serangoon Ave 4
MARCUS TAN
  Singapore
MARCUS TAN ZHI XIANG
  Blk 922 Hougang St 91
MATTHEW AMALAN
  Blk 407 Choa Chu Kang Ave 3
MD NUR AIDIL BIN AHMAD
  Blk 206 Chua Chu Kang Central
MICHELLE YANG
  Blk 114 Bedok Reservoir Rd
MOHD DANIAL BIN MUHD FARUK
  Blk 50 Chai Chee St
MOHD FIRDARUS
  Blk 728 Woodlands Circle
MOHD HASSAN DIN SUPARMAN
  Blk 122E Rivervale Dr
MOHD IMRAN BIN MOHD ARSHAD
  BLK 62 CHAI CHEE RD
MUHAMMAD FIRDAUS
  Blk 286 Choa Chu Kang Ave 3
MUHAMMAD JAKA
  Blk 653C Jurong West St 61
MUHAMMAD RABBANI BIN ROSLI
  Blk 723 Woodlands Ave 6
MUHD RUZAINI BIN ROSMAN
  Blk 103 Bedok North Ave 4
MUHD ZULHIMI RAHMAT
  Blk 323 Ubi Ave 1
N. SAI SRINIRAS
  Blk 217 Bt Batok St 21
NARENDREN
  Blk 425 Choa Chu Kang Ave 4
NASREEN BEGUM
  Blk 107 Potong Pasir Ave 1
NATALIE
  Blk 92 Zion Rd
NATALIE KOH HUI YI
  Blk 213 Serangoon Ave 4
NATALIE TAN ANTING
  Singapore
NG HUI SHAN
  Blk 468 Jurong West St 41

NG HUI YI
Blk 316, Tampines St 33
NG LI JIE
Blk 967 Hougang Ave 9
NG RUI QI
Blk 696 Jurong West Central 1
NG SI MIN CHRISTINE
Blk 567 Hougang St 51
NICHOLAS TAN
Singapore
NICOLE FIONA LAURENS
Blk 681D Woodlands Dr 62
NISHA BTE ABDULLAH
Blk 248 Ang Mo Kio Ave 2
NOOR AMIRAH BTE JAMALLUDIN
Blk 114 Yishun Ring Rd
NUR ASHIKIN BINTE ADBUL KARIM
Blk 682 Hougang Ave 4
NUR FATEHAH BTE SALIM
Blk 81 Redhill Lane
NUR HAZIRAH JUMARI
Blk 456 Tampines St 42
NUR HIDAYAT BIN JASNI
Blk 496F Tampines Ave 9
NUR TASYA UMMAIYAH ZAINAL
Simpang 90-40, Kampung Sengkarai
Tutong TG 5082 Brunei Darulssalam
NURDIYANAH BTE ISMAIL
Blk 774 Bedok Reservoir View
NURSHAFIKAH
Blk 784 Choa Chu Kang Dr
NURSHAMIRAH BTE ADAM
Blk 748 Jurong West St 73
NURUL SYAFIQAH BINTE ABU BAKAR
Blk 323 Sembawang Close
NURUL SYAHIDATUL SYAZWANI
Blk 763 Choa Chu Kang North 5
NURWATI BTE YA'AKOP
Blk 172 Bishan St 13
OLIVIA TANG SHU HUI
Blk 146 Rivervale Dr
ONG SI HUI
Blk 387 Tampines St 32
ONG YI YING
Blk 129, Kim Tian Rd
PAVITHRA D/O GUNASHEKHARAN D
Blk 415 Jurong West St 42
PRIYA D/O DAYALAIN
Blk 423 Ang Mo Kio Ave 3
RACHEL NG
Blk 329 Bt Batok St 33
RACHEL SIAO JIA YU
25 Worthing Rd
RACHEL TEO
Everbright Jaya, Jln Kempas, 93350 Kuching, Sarawak

RAHIMIN BIN RAHIM
Blk 90 Commonwealth Dr
RAHMUNA
Blk 561 Choa Chu Kang North 6
RAHWANI
Blk 561 Choa Chu Kang North 6
RAYMOND TUANG LING XIN
Jln Murni 2, Tmn Mas Merah, Batu Berendam 75350 Melaka
REGINA ONG
Singapore
RONIEL JAY TAN PINEDA
126 Serangoon Ave 3, Golden Heights
RONNIE LAI ZHEN FOONG
Blk 135 Bedok Reservoir Rd
ROWENA LOMBOY GRACIA
Blk 614 Elisa Rd
RU WEI
Singapore
RUBY MANYI CHAN
Lor A5, Taman Satria Jaya BDC Stampin, Kuching Sarawak
S. VIGKNESH
Blk 256 Kim Keat Ave
S. SARAVANNAN
Blk 236 Bt Batok Ave 5
SANDHIKA ADITYADHARMA ADIWIDAJAT
463 Upper East Coast Rd
SANGEETHA D/O BALRAJ
Blk 185A Rivervale Crescent
SARAH LIN ZI LIN
Parkview Apt Tower 3, Bt Batok St 25
SEOW LI TENG ANGELINE
Blk 467 Ang Mo Kio Ave 10
SERAFINA
Singapore
SERENE NG
Blk 348 Bt Batok St 34
SITI NAFSIAH
Blk 48 Bedok South Ave 3
SNG WEI LIANG
Blk 371 Hougang St 31
STEFFI YANIA MOSES
Blk 585 Ang Mo Kio Ave 3
STEPHEN TAN THEAN GEE
Relau Indah Condominium, Persiaran Bt Jambul 1, Pulau Pinang
SWEET NG / MEENA
Blk 769, Yishun Ave 3
TAN BEE ENG
Blk 428 St 41
TAN JING YING
Blk 512 Hougang Ave 10
TAN LIN ER
Blk 773, Bedok Reservoir View

TAN MING FENG
Blk 129 Tampines St 11
TAN WEN YI
Dover Rise, Dover Parkview, Tower C
TAN XUE YING
Blk 610 Choa Chu Kang St 62
TAN YI LING
Blk 511 Ang Mo Kio Ave 8
TAN ZI RUI
Blk 215 Ang Mo Kio Ave1
TAU FIQUE
Blk 10 Eunos Crescent
TEO BAO YING
Blk 765 Jurong West St 74
TEO KAI WEN
Blk 607 Bedok Reservoir Rd
TEO YONG KENG
Blk 256 Serangoon Central Dr
THIO WEN SHUN
Blk 440 Yishun Ave 11
TOH JIA HUI
66 Bayshore Park, Diamond Tower
TRICIA HUI
Blk 173 Bishan St 13
TRIPHTHIPAL SINGH
Blk 922 Jurong West St 92
VANESSA NG QUI RUI
Blk 695 Jurong West Central 1
VANESSA TSAI
Hillwood Rd, Universal Mansion, Kowloon, Hong Kong SAR
VICKI LEONG
Blk 226 Toa Payoh Lorong 8
VINCENT FONG PEI CHERN
Bandar Menjalara, Jln 1/62B, BDR Menjalara, Kuala Lumpur
VISHVANI
Blk 269B Queen Sr
VIVIAN TEO ZHI QING
Geylang Rd Lor 42
WEE LE TING
Blk 99A Cashew Rd Cashew Hts Condo
WEE TUN HOW
Blk 152 Jln Teck Whye
WONG JUN KAI
Blk 548 Serangoon North Ave 3
YEO FENG YU
Blk 12 Joo Seng Rd
YEOW GAN XIN
Blk 542 Choa Chu Kang St 52
YUEN GAH WAI
Blk 613 Chua Chu Kang St 62

Thanks for your email:

Aini • Alan ng • Alex • Alex Lee • Allan Kor • Allen Tan • Angelin Koo • Annie • Anoni Mase • Ashiqah • Belinda Tan • Billy Ong • Boo Quan Wei • Buffy Arfi • Chan Foong Ping • Cheryl • Chong Chai Hong • Christabel Chai • Christina Chua • Chuanlian • Connie Yamada • Conrad Ng • Cool Boy • Daniel Ngee • David Chang • David Lim • Dionis Wee • Dolly Ng • Elizabeth Tan • Elizabeth Tan • Elwin Leong • Emily • Ervin Cheng Shi • Eunice Boon • Evepreet Kaur • Faizal • Fariz Zulhilmi • Fong Liu • Gerald Tan • Gilbert • Gilbert Leow • Grace Goh • Hanis • Harvinpal Singh • Haylie So • Hugo Tan • Isean Tay • Jacqueline Kok • Jamaludin • Jarrod • Jerry Song • Jessica Foo • Jesslyn Chen • Joel Hong • Jonas Tan • Jonathan Kong • Judith Light • Juliana Teoh • Juwi • K Pereira • Kakashi • Kelly Leong • Khoo Yuin Yi • Kimberly • Kimberly San • Kui Liang • Laremie Tan • Lawrence Toh • Lee Yew Chong • Leow Jing Wen • Li Xuan • Lim Jia Yan • Lim Jung Yong • Lim Ming

Jie • Lin Sheng Yen • Low Wan Hoong • Lutfi Haiqal • Lynn Tan • Maris Goh • Md Ross AL Martin Bin Rosman • Md Shukur Ajmaiin • Meera Gal • Michael Tanang King Sing • Michelle Yang • Ming Hui • Mohd Faizal Bin Osman • Monica Robert • Muhd Saifuddin Supandi • Muhd Taufiq, Hidayat & Rahim • Murid Grasio • Naratasha Sari • Ndrea • Ngee Daniel • Nick Tan • Nicol • Nicole Ong • Nicole Oon • Noradibah • Nur Nadiah • Nur Syafiqah Johari • Nurisman • Nurul • Olivier Chen • Ong Ann Aik • Ong Kok Meng • Ovicia • Peggy Yeo • Polin anak Gumbek • Qaaasimy • Rachel Siao • Randolph • Randy Chuah • Raymond Scott Lee Chian Hoong • Richard Woo • Rider Low • Rie Ong Shih Wei • Roy Leow • Rubecca • Ryian Lim • Sam Loh • Sandhika • Sandhika • Sarah Omar • Sarah Ong • Saraphim Teo • Shaun A • Shawn Tay • Shukur • Siklow Hai Ning • Sim Jia Yi • Siti Nuramira • Siu Yuen • Steffi • Sterling • Suraj • Swift leonhart • Tammie • Tan Jia Fang • Tan Li Wen • Tan Teck Wei • Tan Wei Qiang • Tan Yan Rong • Tan Zu De • Tay • Teo Xiao Ting • Teresa Zhou • Tew Chin Heng • Timothy Chan • Tomomi Hikawa • Tong Ong • Veena Vinod • Weng Kee • Weyr • Wui Siew Yen & Children • Xue Xuan • Yan Rong • Yeo Jing Ying

Please do include your contact details in all your letters. With email, sending stories in is really easy. So send in as many stories as you wish.

Take care and write soon!

russelllee@flameoftheforest.com

CONTENTS

PART I

Hungry Uncle Henry   18

A SPECIAL STORY
Love potion Number 10   22
A step out of line   24
Friday the 13th   26
Angel of death   27

A SPECIAL STORY
Nina and the dwarf kingdom   30

PART II

RUSSELL LEE INVESTIGATES:
LIFE AFTER DEATH

Near-death experiences   36
Suicide — not the way to go   39
A funny side   40
Pain and suffering   40
Heaven   41
Hell   42
Purgatory   45
Reincarnation   45

A SPECIAL STORY
Pact with the Devil   48

PART III

A SPECIAL STORY
Saved by a cross   53
How to see a ghost   61
Manchester United forever   62

A SPECIAL STORY
The littlest angel   65
Ghost marriage   67

PART IV

RUSSELL LEE INTERVIEWS
MAIA LEE
My unwanted gift   71
Trip to China   73
Fire hazard   74
View from my room   75
Losing myself   75
The Yamaha organ   76
Naked man of Block 107   77
Closing the third eye   78

RUSSELL LEE INTERVIEWS
WINONA WEE
My new friend   79

PART V

A SPECIAL STORY
The jealous ghost   85
A mother's love   89

Army daze   90
Charm soup for a young man   95
Vale of tempe   97
Naughty baby   100
My homesick uncle   101
Not a technical problem   104
The ghost of Newton Circus   106
Room with a view   108
Hot in Geylang   112
Ghost of Bus 854   115
Handphone message   117
Tsunami ghost   118
My best friend   120
Hantu raya   125
The disappearing dolls   127

A SPECIAL STORY
Fear of flying   129

PART VI

A SPECIAL STORY
The poker king   134

A SPECIAL STORY
Bishan Park after dark   139
Bride from Hell   141
The thieving toyol   146

A SPECIAL STORY
A-li-shan de gu niang   149

THE ANGSANA RUSSELL LEE
WRITERS' CONTEST (BOOK 13)   159

PART I

HUNGRY UNCLE HENRY

Roland Lim, 20, national serviceman

They say the way to a man's heart is through his stomach. Well, that was certainly true for my dear departed Uncle Henry. His wife Cheryl loved him with all her heart and soul.

All his friends remarked that Uncle Henry was a very lucky man to marry Aunt Cheryl. Blessed with charm and poise, she has a warm and vibrant personality. She can light up any room with her stately and dignified presence.

And to top it all, her culinary skills are unmatched. Chinese barbecued baby back ribs, a full spread of Malay nasi padang, succulent T-bone steaks with yummy baked potatoes and even tender tandoori chicken is no problem for her.

Her repertoire of dishes is so remarkable that I think she would have made a small fortune if she had opened a restaurant. But Aunt Cheryl was more than contented to be a happy housewife.

Uncle Henry would often tease her about how she "conned" him into marrying her.

"You know," he would say, "I had so many girls vying for my attention but none would cook and bring food out in a Tupperware for me like your aunt. It came to a point when I looked forward to the food more than seeing her."

He was joking, of course. Aunt Cheryl was not one for resting on her laurels and her skills improved over the years. Little wonder then that all family gatherings were held at Uncle Henry's.

There would always be a sumptuous spread whenever the family met and I looked forward to these gatherings. It was a time to play with all my cousins and eat to my heart's content.

"Mum, why can't you cook like Aunt Cheryl?" I asked Mum once.

"It's a good thing I can't or you'd be a fat little boy," she replied with a straight face.

To a certain extent, I guess it's true. My cousins Melvin and Jenny are, to put it nicely, on the wrong end of the weighing scale.

From Uncle Henry's wedding photos, I know that he was an athletic and handsome young man. But as the years passed, his friends nicknamed him "Samo" after the rotund Hong Kong action star Samo Hung.

I was very fond of Uncle Henry. He had a good sense of humour. Knowing I supported Arsenal, he would faithfully buy me their latest replica kits and, on my birthdays, he would buy me the latest Arsenal memorabilia.

On my 16th birthday, he gave me a football, with Thierry Henry's signature, which his friend brought back from London.

Tragically, Uncle Henry died two years ago in a car accident after a drunk driver mowed him down while he was crossing the road.

Aunt Cheryl and the kids were devastated. Mum, who is Uncle Henry's elder sister, couldn't stop crying for days.

Aunt Cheryl put on a brave front and soldiered on. She did her best for Melvin and Jenny, showering them with extra love and care. Still, things were never the same without Uncle Henry and Aunt Cheryl's anguish was plain for all to see.

A Buddhist, she went to the temple to pray for his soul and burnt paper offerings and hell bank notes to ensure that he'd have a good life in the netherworld.

When the Hungry Ghost Festival came around, she diligently prepared his favourite dishes and laid it out on the dining table.

The Hungry Ghost Festival begins on the seventh day of the seventh month in the lunar calendar and it lasts for a month. For one month, the gates of hell remain open for hungry ghosts to roam the earth and to be fed.

We visited Aunt Cheryl on the first day of the Hungry Ghost Festival. She said some prayers and asked Uncle Henry to take his fill of the food. Ghosts feed on the "essence" of the food and leave the rest behind. But Aunt Cheryl had no appetite and her children did not believe in the custom.

My parents and I politely declined because we are Christians and didn't feel it was appropriate. Aunt Cheryl didn't mind. She seemed grateful just having us there.

She reminisced about the good times with Uncle Henry and we listened with more than a tinge of sadness. When we left a few hours later, Uncle Henry filled our thoughts. The next morning, my mother told me that an excited Aunt Cheryl had called.

Apparently, Uncle Henry had "returned" the night before!

"Auntie Cheryl is convinced that Uncle Henry

came home," said Mum.

"How does she know?" I asked.

"Because he ate his favourite chicken wings," Mum said.

You see, Aunt Cheryl had cooked Hainanese chicken rice and when she woke up to clear the food, she noticed that both chicken wings were gone! We all knew that when he was alive, Uncle Henry loved his chicken wings. Aunt Cheryl would fry them by the dozen to satisfy him.

We went over to Aunt Cheryl's again that same evening and she showed us the plate of chicken, with just the wings missing!

The children swore that they had not touched them. It was Jenny, who was 12 then, who first noticed the missing wings.

"Mummy, Mummy, Daddy came home!" she cried out. "He's still thinking about us."

Tears welled in Aunt Cheryl's eyes as she replied, "Yes, darling. Daddy misses us as much as we miss him."

And although Aunt Cheryl prepared various chicken dishes over the Hungry Ghost Festival, the food was never touched again.

It may have been a coincidence but Uncle Henry appeared to his beloved wife in a dream on the last night of the Hungry Ghost Festival.

"It was so vivid," Aunt Cheryl told us. "In the dream, Henry held my hand and told me that he missed me and the children very much. He said he was happy where he was and told me not to worry about him."

"I felt relieved to hear that," she said. "He also

said that he knew we would be reunited one day. And you know what? He even said that the Hainanese chicken rice I cooked that day was a bit too salty. It's just like him to be cheeky."

We all laughed when we heard that. Bon appetit, Uncle Henry!

A SPECIAL STORY

LOVE POTION NUMBER 10

Fanny Yong, 46, teacher

I believe that many readers would have heard the catchy classic song "Love Potion No 9" before. It is also the title of an old movie based on the premise of a love potion making one irresistible to the opposite sex.

In Sabah, where I live, some ethnic groups still believe in the power of black magic in matters of love. Some still consult a traditional medicine man, known as a bomoh, when they get sick or when they want to win someone's heart through unethical means.

My colleague, Antinius, who is a Kadazandusun, told me the following true story. Tina, his beautiful niece, was once charmed by a man whom she truly detested.

Tina was 18 then. Gentle and pretty, she once participated in a harvest festival beauty pageant and won first prize. She was the most attractive girl in the village and although many young men tried to woo her, she simply wasn't interested. Tina's burning ambition was to further her studies and she worked part-time as a waitress to save up for her education.

One of her ardent suitors was Sam, a colleague from the restaurant. However, Sam was addicted to "ubat batuk", cough syrup containing codeine.

As you'd expect, Tina avoided him like the plague. On top of his dubious moral values, his personal hygiene standards left much to be desired. But this cunning fellow approached his bomoh uncle to help him win Tina's heart. The bomoh concocted a very potent love potion, which Sam secretly put in Tina's lunch when she went to the toilet.

This is why sometimes our elders insist that a woman should never leave her food unguarded.

After she had eaten her food, Tina acted as if she had lost her mind. To her parents' dismay, she started seeing Sam regularly.

In those days, it was socially and culturally inappropriate for a maiden like Tina to see a man without a chaperone. She behaved like a lovesick damsel. Once, she even rushed to his house during a midnight thunderstorm, just because he needed some money to feed his drug habit.

Friends couldn't understand why she would risk her reputation for the sake of an unemployed junkie with a criminal record.

Her mother, close to her wits' end, consulted a bobohizan, a Kadazandusun high priestess. The high priestess, discerning that she had been charmed, taught her the way to break the spell.

It entailed the use of smelly pig feed, consisting of rotten vegetables, stale food and bones.

Tina's mother went to a farmer to buy the stuff. One afternoon, she deliberately dropped a spoon on the ground and asked Tina to pick it up.

While her daughter was bending down, she poured the pail of pig feed all over Tina, as she had been instructed to.

Caught unawares and covered from head to toe with the revolting mixture, Tina vomited violently. Her mother then dragged her to the river and gave her a good scrubbing.

The following day, when that scumbag came to woo her, she cursed him and threatened to report him to the penghulu, the village headman. She wouldn't be caught dead being seen with him, let alone marry him!

The spell was well and truly broken.

Russell Lee: I guess on a scale of one to 10, the evil bomoh's brew scored a Love Potion Number 10!

A STEP OUT OF LINE

Charlene Wong, 10, student

If you look very carefully, you'll notice a wooden divider at the front door of most Buddhist temples. Don't step on the divider as it's considered rude. Some of my friends laugh this off, dismissing it as mere superstition.

As I'm hardly the temple-going type, I forget

these unwritten temple rules and I have to be reminded often.

Recently, I was in Kuching, East Malaysia, for a holiday. While there, my elder cousin took me to a temple to pray.

I noticed the thick wooden divider on the floor. Without thinking, I stepped on the divider, even after my cousin had warned me not to.

After saying the usual prayers, we returned home. My cousin's father returned at about the same time and parked his motorbike next to the front gate.

My cousin's sister was soon home as well and she jumped on the motorbike playfully. She pretended to ride the bike, imagining she was in a race. It was fun and I wanted to join her so I sat next to her but my leg accidentally brushed against the flaming hot exhaust pipe.

It hurt as much as a dozen bee stings combined and I winced in pain, unable to control my tears. I wondered if God was displeased with me for being rude in stepping on the divider?

Russell, since you are so experienced in the supernatural stuff, can you tell me if God has forgiven me?

And, by the way, please warn your readers (if they are Buddhists) not to step on the wooden divider at temple entrances in case something similar happens to them.

Russell Lee: I'm sure that what happened on the motorbike was just an accident since you were not delib-

erately rude. God doesn't get angry with kids with no ill intentions.

FRIDAY THE 13TH

Alvin Tay, 13, student

Has anything unlucky ever happened to you on Friday the 13th, Russell?

It is common folklore that it is bad luck to go out on Friday the 13th but I'm not a superstitious person. I love playing basketball and I'm on the school team.

Whenever I can, I go to a basketball court near my house to practise.

On Friday, May 13, 2005, I was getting ready to go to the court to sharpen my skills for a coming basketball match.

As I was about to step out of the house, my grandfather told me not to go out as it was Friday the 13th.

I told him not to worry. Upon reaching the court, I warmed up before shooting some hoops. I was playing happily on my own when something strange happened an hour later.

As I was in the middle of a jump shot, I suddenly felt a cold hand pulling me down. It felt as if an opponent was trying to prevent me from shooting.

I lost my balance in mid-air and fell to the ground.

Instead of feeling embarassed, I felt frightened. I dismissed it as my imagination and continued playing.

But it happened again. This time, it wasn't pulling at my singlet but slapping my hands.

It was a deliberate foul. But who was my opponent?

I quickly grabbed my ball and ran back home.

I have read all your books, Russell, but I have never come across a ghost who likes playing basketball. Do you think that ghosts like sports, too, Russell?

Russell Lee: Yes, I do. In Book 11, ex-Singapore footballer V Sundramoorthy tells about a bunch of ghosts happily playing football. I'm not a huge fan of basketball but I'd like to visit you some time and see if I can go one-on-one with your mystery opponent.

ANGEL OF DEATH

Astla Esmael, 16, student

For the last three years, I've been suffering and I hope you can help me, Russell.

I believe that I've come face to face with an angel of death. And it scares me.

Let me tell you a little more about myself. After the death of my dad and my grandpa, I felt lost and lonely because I was close to both of them.

About a week before my grandfather died, I had begun to feel uneasy. I had the premonition that I was going to lose someone.

One night, I was in my room trying to get some rest. I slipped into a fitful sleep. All of a sudden, I could see the figure of a man — an elderly man wearing a white jubah, the robes that many Arab men wear especially when doing their prayers.

He was standing right in front of me. I couldn't really see his face. Without any reason, I began to cry.

I felt afraid even though he didn't do anything to hurt me. When I tried to look at his face, I found myself staring into a bright light.

"I'll be coming again soon," he said in Arabic. "*Ba aragah lak phil qareeb.*" He then vanished.

When I told Mum about it, she said I must have been dreaming. But I had the feeling that something bad was about to happen. Exactly a week later, my grandpa passed away peacefully.

When we buried him, I saw the elderly man who had appeared before me! He was standing over the grave. I looked around but no one else seemed to have seen him even though he was right in front of my eyes.

Later, I told my aunt and uncle about it and they told me that maybe I had seen an "angel of death".

It has happened a few times. A few months later, in 2003, I saw that old man again a week before my aunt, my mum's sister, died.

And in January 2004, I saw him again a week before my favourite uncle passed on. I cried every time I met him as I knew that he was a harbinger of death and sorrow.

I've read about the Grim Reaper, the skeleton in a black cloak carrying a scythe coming to claim souls. It's scary and I much rather that an angel escort a departing soul. The thing I don't understand is why the old man chose to break the bad news to me first.

Now my mother believes me when I tell her about the mysterious figure. Honestly, I don't know when all this is going to end.

In July 2004, my grandmother was in critical condition. All my uncles and aunts came to my house to see her.

It was about 10.45 pm when that familiar presence appeared before me again.

"Oh no, not again!" I thought to myself. I felt sure he was going to take my grandmother away. I pleaded with him to give her more time because she wanted to see one of my cousins getting married in February 2005.

I pleaded with much tears. As usual, he hardly said a word but appeared to nod his head.

Maybe he took pity on me. Till today, my grandmother is still alive. She witnessed the wedding of my cousin and I enjoyed watching her laugh and taking part in everything. Life, how precious it is. I am grateful for every breath, for every additional minute that I live on this earth.

I pray that I will not see the "angel of death" again. Everyone has to die. I just do not want to know when.

A SPECIAL STORY

NINA AND THE DWARF KINGDOM

Hamidah Bachok, 34, human resource manager

Russell, do you believe in dwarves? As in *Snow White and the Seven Dwarves?* I do. My mother Nina met them and told me all about it.

This happened in the 1950s when my mother was a teenager. Her grandparents brought her up and they stayed in a very remote village in the Pasir Ris area.

Her grandfather was a bomoh and all the villagers knew him for he was both very fierce and very brave. Mother was a striking beauty when she was young, and many admired her. However, villagers were wary of her as they knew her grandfather's temper all too well.

Anyway, in those days, villagers had to use wells as their water source. And when they had to bathe or wash their clothes, they used nearby rivers. At around nine in the morning one day, my mother walked to the river to bathe. Her house was only about 500 metres from the river.

But that morning, it seemed like five kilometres. My mother kept following the pathway and wondered why she still hadn't reached the river banks. It seemed to her that she had walked for ages before she found herself in a place which was totally new to her. She eventually called it "the dwarf kingdom".

It was a very special and unique place. It was

filled with grand palaces and the city was a bustling hive of activity.

Mother said it was similar to our world. There were even lawyers and doctors, cars, schools, offices and everyone seemed to be well dressed!

There was one difference. The inhabitants of this kingdom were all only about three feet tall! The men were bearded and had rather large noses. The women were shy and giggly when they saw my mother.

A kind-hearted guy, who introduced himself as Humble, offered her a tour around the city.

My mother later referred to him as her "dear friend". After the sightseeing, he invited her over to his home. It was the largest and grandest place in the city. It was the king's palace as Humble belonged to the royal family!

She was welcomed by his family and they entertained her with a grand banquet. To this day, my mother says it was the best meal of her life.

The table was laden with all sorts of meat, salads and fruits prepared by the royal chef.

There were servants waiting on them hand and foot and it was a proper formal affair.

Humble's family members were nice and they seemed fond of her. When they were about to eat, Humble told my mother that there were two types of rice on the table, black and white.

If my mother were to eat the black rice, she would not be able to go back home. She would have to remain with the dwarves forever.

She would be provided with a grand palace of

her own and have anything her heart desired in the dwarf kingdom.

If, however, she chose the white rice, she would have to leave the dwarf kingdom. My mother felt at home among the kind dwarves and the glittering riches were tempting. But the thought of her grandparents made her reach for the white rice.

They chatted happily over their meal. When they were done, Humble walked her around the palace. Glittering diamonds and precious stones adorned the walls.

Meanwhile, it was already night and her grandparents were getting worried. They combed the whole area but there was no trace of her.

Since there was no sign of my mother, her grandfather suspected something was amiss and he gathered a number of men and surrounded the big old tree near the path on the way to the river.

He knew about the dwarf kingdom. Her grandfather shouted loudly for the dwarves to return my mother, Nina.

Humble heard Grandfather's cries and asked Mother to return. Suddenly, my mother found herself under the big old tree, surrounded by the village folk.

My mother was wondering why it was already night. It seemed like she had only been away for a short time. The following day, the villagers told my mother that she was lucky to be able to leave. It seemed that there were other young women who went missing and were never found. The villagers believed that the big tree was the entrance to the dwarf world.

Perhaps the dwarves took a fancy to human women and wanted to make them their wives. Who knows? Maybe Humble had taken a liking to my mother.

Till today, my mother cannot forget her encounter with the dwarves. She's also thankful to Humble for telling her the difference between eating the black and white rice. Imagine what would have happened if Mother had eaten the black rice instead of the white.

She has fond memories of Humble and of her time with the dwarves.

Sometimes, my father and I tease her about giving up her chance to be Snow White in the dwarf kingdom!

Russell Lee: This story reminds me of the story, "Puaka People", in Book 10, about tiny beings the size of Coca-Cola bottles.

PART II

RUSSELL LEE INVESTIGATES:
LIFE AFTER DEATH

An American journalist once wrote, "Death is but a distant rumour to the young."

That is certainly true in my case. When I was young, many carefree days were spent playing football and having fun with my friends. My biggest worry was the end-of-year examinations.

While I don't have a morbid fascination phobia with it, the subject of death is certainly more real to me today than when I was a teen.

I have attended the funerals of people close to me and I certainly hope that they are in a better place. One quote that captivates me is "You can be a king or a street sweeper, but everybody dances with the Grim Reaper". Those were the last words of convicted murderer Robert Alton Harris before he was executed in the gas chamber in 1992.

That set me thinking. Death is indeed the great leveller. You may be the richest man in the world but you can't take your wealth with you into the grave. On the other hand, you might die a penniless beggar. As the Johnny Cash song, "Country Trash", goes: "We'll all be equal under the grass".

But is death a point in a journey or the end of that journey? Scientists don't have the answer. After all, they will not find out until they die. And when they do, they will be not be around to report their findings.

Philosophers differ in their opinions on life after death while theologians have varying theories.

Will you go to heaven? Is there a hell? Or will

you be reincarnated as a prince or princess or maybe even return as a pig or a rat?

Or does life, as we know it, end when we breathe our last, beyond which there is no existence? There are some who subscribe to this philosophy. During a discussion, a friend of mine said, "Hey, Russell, life is short. Enjoy it while you can. This is as good as it gets."

He didn't believe in life after death. He felt that we would all return to a state of "nothingness".

But I don't believe it's as simple as that.

Everyone is shaped by his or her own spiritual experiences. If you ask me whether I believe in life after death, my answer is "yes".

What will it be like? I honestly don't know. But I have my own beliefs on what awaits us. In the meantime, I will try and spread as much love, joy, peace and understanding as I can.

In the following pages, I will explore the possible scenarios of life after death.

Near-death experiences

This is a phenomenon reported by some people who have been pronounced clinically dead, then returned to life.

Descriptions of the experience differ slightly in detail from person to person, but usually share some basic elements: A feeling of being outside one's body, a sensation of sliding down a long tunnel, and the appearance of a bright light at the end of that tunnel.

Thousands of near-death experience (NDE) stories abound on the Internet but I will look at the NDEs of the rich and famous, in particular.

Celebrities who have had a glimpse of the afterlife include Sharon Stone, Jane Seymour, Peter Sellers, Elizabeth Taylor, Larry Hagman, Eric Estrada, Rebecca DeMornay, Chevy Chase and *Star Wars* creator George Lucas.

They have come out publicly about their experiences with nothing to gain. They are already rich and famous. In fact, by telling everyone that they came back from the dead, they may have been risking their own reputations.

People who reveal such things often become the butt of jokes or are thought to be crazy. So why would these stars subject themselves to this?

The only rational reason is that it happened to them and they want to share it.

Movie star Sharon Stone, best known for her role in *Basic Instinct,* almost died in 2001 after suffering a brain haemorrhage. "I was haemorrhaging in my brain for 11 days before they found out what was wrong," she said.

On her NDE, she said, "This kind of giant vortex of white light was upon me and I kind of — *poof* — sort of took off into this glorious, bright, bright, bright, white light and I started to see and be met by some of my beloved family and friends.

"But it was very fast, *whoosh!* Suddenly, I was back. I was in my body and I was in the room. I had a real journey with this that took me to places both here and beyond that affected me so profoundly that my life will never be the same.

"I've always been a spiritual person and it's clear to me that God has a plan and a purpose for me. I walk in the joy and ease of that."

Few people know that legendary Hollywood star Elizabeth Taylor was once pronounced clinically dead while undergoing surgery. She disclosed that she passed through a tunnel towards a brilliant white light.

Interviewed by Larry King on CNN's *Larry King Live,* the legendary Hollywood star related how she had "died" for five minutes on the operating table.

She said, "I was pronounced dead once and actually saw the light. I find it very hard to talk about, actually, because it sounds so corny."

Taylor said that while she was clinically dead, she had encountered the spirit of Michael Todd, one of her former husbands, whom she referred to as her "great love".

She had wanted to stay with Todd, she said, but he had told her that she had work and life ahead of her, and he "pushed me back to my life".

She added, "When I came to, there were about 11 people in the room. I'd been gone for about five minutes; they had given me up for dead and put my death notice on the wall.

"For a long time I didn't talk about it, and it is still hard for me to talk about. But I have shared it with people with Aids. I'm not afraid of death, because I've been there."

Many celebrities' accounts have been documented in Jean Ritchie's *Death's Door.*

Skeptics explain off the NDE as a kind of defence mechanism that our mind uses to protect us and help us cope with death. The brain creates this near-death illusion, and in doing so helps us deal with impending death.

Thousands and thousands of people have claimed to experience NDEs. Many are grateful for the second chance and have gone about life with greater purpose, determined to make every second count.

Suicide – not the way to go

People who attempted suicide but failed experience confusion and torment instead of relief and happiness.

"If you leave life with a restless soul, then you will arrive into the other world with a restless soul," says a specialist in the field of suicide.

Suicide victims commit suicide to "end it all", but, as it happens, it is only their beginning in the other world.

One man, who loved his wife dearly, killed himself when she died. He hoped to reunite with her for eternity, but things turned out quite differently. When the doctor revived him, he said, "I was in a place quite different from where she was… It was a dreadful place… and immediately I realised that I had made a huge mistake."

Some revived suicide victims describe arriving in a kind of prison or dungeon where they feel that they will have to remain for a very long time. They recognise that this is their punishment for violating the established law, which requires that each person must suffer his share of sorrows.

Having wilfully thrown off the burdens placed upon them, they must carry even more in the world to come.

A funny side

I read this humorous piece and thought I'd share it with you guys.

A middle-aged woman has a heart attack and is taken to the hospital. While on the operating table she has a near-death experience. During that experience she sees God and asks if this is it. God says no and explains that she has another 30 to 40 years to live. Upon her recovery she decides to just stay in the hospital and have a facelift, liposuction, tummy tuck, the works.

She even has someone come in and change her hair colour. She figures since she's got another 30 or 40 years she might as well make the most of it. She walks out the hospital after the last operation and is killed by an ambulance speeding up to the hospital.

She arrives in front of God and asks, "I thought you said I had another 30 to 40 years to live?" God replies, "I'm sorry, I didn't recognise you."

Pain and suffering

On a more serious note, there is no denying that pain and suffering is everywhere around us. People with critical illnesses and physical disabilities carry a burden that is unimaginable to the healthy person.

Likewise, those who have suffered great psychological trauma carry a different kind of burden on their shoulders.

Everyone, to a certain extent, has tasted suffering. So is a life without pain imaginable?

Heaven

Followers of Christianity and Islam, two of the world's major religions, believe in the concept of heaven and hell.

The Bible says that "no eye has seen, no ear has heard, no mind has conceived what God has prepared for those who love Him".

There is no sorrow or death or pain in heaven. Instead, there will be laughter and rejoicing.

One thing is for sure, there will be no poverty in heaven either. The city streets of heaven will be made of pure gold, as described in Revelation.

Born-again Christians believe that Jesus has prepared many mansions in heaven and at the right time, Jesus will return to bring them there.

In Islam, there are different views held by different sects or Muslim scholars. The general understanding tends to perceive the otherworldly form as very similar to the one here on earth.

Heaven or paradise is presented as an immeasurably large garden literally abounding in beautiful trees casting eternal shadows under which rivers will flow.

The rivers will be of milk and honey. The garden will be filled with fruit-bearing trees and the meat will be from all sorts of birds.

Female companions of exceeding beauty and refinement would be provided to the pious men, with no limit imposed on the number, which will be decided according to their capacity. As many as they can cope with will be theirs.

The enjoyment therefore is sensual. No work to be performed, no labour to be wasted, no effort to be made.

Reclining on heavenly cushions of silk and brocade, dwellers will while their time away in eternal bliss.

But there are others who categorically reject this understanding and prove with many references to verses of the *Holy Quran* that what it describes is just metaphorical imagery which has no carnality about it.

In fact, they say, the *Holy Quran* makes it amply clear that the form of existence of the life to come will be so different from all known forms of life here on earth, that it is beyond human imagination even to have the slightest glimpse of the otherworldly realities.

"We will raise you into a form of which you have not the slightest knowledge," says Surah Al-Waqiah (56: 62).

Hell

Over here in Singapore, many working adults chase after the 5Cs — namely, cash, credit card, car, condominium and country club membership.

The last thing on their mind is Judgement Day. But the *Bible* and *Quran* state that every man will have to be accountable to his Maker after death.

Several years ago, a book entitled *Beyond Death's Door* by Dr Maurice Rawlings, was published. Dr Rawlings, a specialist in Internal Medicine and Cardiovascular Disease, resuscitated many people who had been clinically dead.

Dr Rawlings, a devout atheist, had considered all religions "hocus-pocus" and death nothing more than a "painless extinction".

But something happened in 1977 that changed his thinking. He was resuscitating a man who was terrified and screaming while descending into the flames of hell!

In his book, Dr Rawlings described the incident: "Each time he regained his heartbeat and respiration, the patient screamed, 'I am in hell!'

"He was terrified and pleaded with me to help him. I was scared to death. Then I noticed a genuinely alarmed look on his face. He had a terrified look worse than the expression seen in death.

"This patient had a grotesque grimace expressing sheer horror. His pupils were dilated and he was perspiring and trembling. He looked as if his hair was standing on end.

"He shouted, 'Don't you understand? I am in hell... Don't let me go back to hell.' The man was serious and it finally occurred to me that he was indeed in trouble. He was in a panic like I had never seen before."

Dr Rawlings said no one, who could have heard the man's screams and saw the look of terror on his face, could doubt for a single minute that he was actually in a place called hell.

Some of the words used to describe hell in the *Bible* are "everlasting fire", "everlasting punishment", "everlasting chains", "blackness of darkness forever" and a place where there is much weeping, wailing and gnashing of teeth.

There are also a huge number of Quranic references to hell. Some of the punishments include being beaten with rods, iron, or a chain of 70 cubits, boiling springs, burning despair and ice-cold darkness, fire burning on one's face, scorching, choking on liquid pus, and being tortured with sores and thorns.

It is hard to imagine how intolerable hell will be and the concept of an eternity in it. The following story will help to put things in perspective.

An enfeebled man, after suffering for many years, finally prayed to the Lord for an end to his suffering. An angel appeared to him and said, "Your sins require cleansing. The Lord offers you to exchange one year of suffering on earth for three hours of hell. Choose."

The sufferer contemplated his choices and decided on three hours in hell. Then the angel took him into the pit of hell. All around was darkness, narrowness, evil spirits, the cries of sinners, and suffering.

The soul of the enfeebled began to experience indescribable fear and pain, but only echoes and the surging hellfire answered his screams. No one noticed his groans and bellows; all of the sinners were occupied with their own suffering.

The sufferer felt that centuries had passed and that the angel had forgotten him. Finally, the angel appeared to him and asked, "Well, how are you, brother?"

"You tricked me!" exclaimed the sufferer. "Not three hours, but many years I have been here in intolerable pain!"

"What years?" the angel asked. "Only an hour has passed, and you still have two to go."

Then the sufferer begged the angel to return

him to earth where he was willing to suffer as many years as required, if only to leave this place of terrors.

"Very well," answered the angel, "the Lord will show His Great Mercy." Finding himself back on his sickbed, the sufferer, from that point forward, bore his sufferings with meekness, always remembering hell's terrors, which are incomparably worse (from the letters of Sviatogortz, Pg 183, 15th letter, 1883).

Purgatory

From the Latin word "purgare", meaning to make clean or to purify, Purgatory is believed by Roman Catholics to be a place or condition of temporal punishment.

It has traditionally been viewed as a place of torment with excruciating fires.

Gregory the Great wrote "that the pain be more intolerable than anyone can suffer in this life". Augustine and St Bonaventure agreed.

The purpose of this pain is to purify the individual. Eventually, the person will be cleansed and be eligible to be transferred to Heaven.

One writer comments, "Which of us does not tremble when he thinks of those who have been burnt to death in a slow fire? Yet their suffering was of relatively short duration.

"The incomparably fiercer fire of Purgatory, which we may have to face, may last 20 or 50 or 100 years!"

Reincarnation

Reincarnation is the belief that one is reborn

in another body at the point of death.

It is the belief that one has lived before and will live again in another body. The bodies one passes in and out of need not be human.

One may have been a Doberman in a past life, and one may be a mite or a grasshopper in a future life. Some people avoid eating certain animals because they believe that the souls of their ancestors dwell in those animals.

Ancient Egyptians believed in reincarnation, or transmigration of the soul, and embalmed the body in order to preserve it. This was to allow the body to journey along with the soul to the next world or life.

A recent survey showed that almost one in four Americans believe in reincarnation. The percentage should be higher in Asian culture.

Buddhists regard rebirth as a fact, believing that each person has lived many lives in the past and will continue to live more lives in the future.

In recent years, much research has been done on the possibility of rebirth. The case of Bridey Murphy is well-documented.

Mrs Ruth Simmons of the United States recollected a previous life in Ireland, more than 100 years ago. She said she had been Bridey Murphy in the year 1789 and gave full details of Bridey's life. The details were later checked and found to be quite accurate although, in her present life, Mrs Simmons had never been outside the US.

In Buddhism, there are six realms in which one may be reborn after death. They are the realms of gods, the demigods, human beings, animals, hungry ghosts and hell beings.

The realm into which one is reborn and one's conditions of rebirth are determined by one's past and present actions. This is the law of karma where positive, caring actions will bring positive results back to you while negative, hurtful actions will result in suffering.

In other words, you reap what you sow or what goes around comes around.

The concept of karma is common to both Buddhism and Hinduism.

Hindus believe that the soul is immortal and is reincarnated in a new body after a person dies. Thus, you have an endless series of lives to work on your karma. In each life, you should strive to do good works and evolve spiritually so your next life will be better than the previous one.

Hindus seek to eventually break free of the cycle of reincarnation and attain eternal bliss of the soul, called moksha. But one can go through millions of reincarnations before moksha.

During these reincarnations, one can evolve into a higher or lower form of life (for example, as a plant, tree or animal). Hopefully, one will eventually work off all the bad karma and attain unity with the divine.

When one attains moksha, there is no need for further reincarnation.

In Buddhism, the ultimate goal is to reach Nibbana or Nirvana.

Buddha reached the state of Nirvana during his enlightenment. Nirvana literally means extinguishing or unbinding. When one finds complete freedom from desire, jealousy and ignorance, a state of bliss is achieved.

There is no longer the need for the cycle of birth and death.

Life is fragile. Let's live it as fully as we can, while we can. The next story is from a reader who genuinely has an ominous fear of life after death.

A SPECIAL STORY

PACT WITH THE DEVIL

Sunny Quek, 67, retired architect

I guess I'm one of the oldest to write in. I saw you promoting *True Singapore Ghost Stories Book 12* at a Popular outlet in Toa Payoh one day, Russell, and I decided to get a copy.

I found your stories entertaining. As I grow older day by day, I often think about life after death.

When one is young, death is not a thought that frequently comes to mind. There are those who say they are not afraid to die but the thought terrifies me.

Life has been good to me. I made my money during the construction boom in the 1970s and 1980s. I live in a big bungalow at Watten Estate and a chauffeur ferries me around in a Jaguar.

I have a few million dollars in my bank account and properties in Singapore, Malaysia and Australia.

But I'm afraid that my success has come at too high a price. It may have cost me my soul.

You see, Russell, I made a pact with the devil when I was young. I agreed to sell him my soul in return for everything my heart desired.

Like many others in the post-war era, my family was not well-to-do. My father was a clerk while my mother was a seamstress.

I vowed one day that I would make my mark in the world. When I was 20, I worked as a draughtsman in a British firm. I fancied a beautiful girl who worked there as a secretary.

One day, I expressed my desire to be her boyfriend. I did not get the answer I was hoping for.

She started laughing and told me to take a good look at myself in the mirror. "I can pick who I like to be my boyfriend," she said. "There are many men wooing me. You are just a poor, lowly draughtsman. You don't even own a car. You are the last person I would choose."

That episode left me very bitter. Even though I wasn't a religious person, I went home and prayed to God to make me a rich man.

Months passed and nothing changed. Meanwhile, Fanny, the secretary, had found herself a boyfriend. He was the son of a rich businessman and he picked her from work every day in a big, black shiny sports car.

I burned with envy at the sight of them together. "If God won't help me, maybe the devil will," I thought to myself.

So I made a plea to the devil, telling him that I would exchange my soul for material wealth.

A voice in my head seemed to say, "Are you absolutely sure? Selling me your soul is no laughing matter."

I then made the biggest mistake of my life. I kneeled down in my room and said a silent "prayer". I remember saying, "If there really is a devil, I pledge my soul to you if you will help me to get rich."

I fell asleep very troubled but almost overnight, doors started opening for me.

My boss told me that I had impressed him with my work and that he would sponsor my education in Australia. After four years abroad, I returned home with an architecture degree.

Grateful to my boss, I worked hard for him for the next five years. I had always been an introvert but I was suddenly given a glib tongue.

I helped him clinch many contracts and more than repaid him what he had forked out for my education. In return, he rewarded me handsomely with a portion of the company's profits.

I finally decided to strike it out on my own, so I opened a small firm. Everything I touched seem to turn into gold.

By the time I turned 40, I had offices in Singapore, Kuala Lumpur, Brunei and Kuching.

Life couldn't have been better. I married a former beauty queen and have two adorable kids.

All my friends remarked that my luck was incredible. There was turmoil all around in the world but I could never empathise because I felt untouchable. But time flies when you're having a good time. As the years have gone by, my hairline has been steadily receding and the wrinkles have grown more pronounced. Painful bouts with arthritis leave me all too aware of my mortality.

I had almost forgotten my pact with the devil, attributing all my good fortune to my hard work.

But I was reminded of that fateful night so many years ago when I attended the funeral of my close friend Simon. Looking into the casket to pay my respects, a vision suddenly flashed before me. Instead of Simon's face, I saw my own face!

A devilishly handsome creature appeared in my mind and said, "Your time is running out, Sunny. I look forward to seeing you soon."

I had always slept soundly but nightmares have begun to torment me. I dream of flames and an unquenchable thirst.

They are so real that I always wake up in a cold sweat. I have begun going to temples and churches even though I've never been a religious person. In the hope of redemption, I've even started to give generously to charities.

But till today, I cannot find peace of mind.

I still patronise the finest restaurants and live in the poshest suites when I travel. But somehow, it's all meaningless and do not have the same allure that they did when I was young.

If possible, I would trade all my material trappings for peace of mind and sound sleep.

But it may all be too late I fear.

Russell Lee: It's never too late to repent.

PART III

A SPECIAL STORY

SAVED BY A CROSS

Lauryn Tze, 17, unemployed

I failed my "O" levels last year. My parents want me to repeat them this year but, honestly, I don't see the point in trying. After all, my parents care for my two younger brothers more than me.

You may ask how I know, Russell... it's my own family, so I sure know!

Anyway, I told them I'd get a job and they didn't object too much. I could see they couldn't wait to get me out of their house. Well, as soon as I start to earn my own money, I'm moving out! I'm sick of it all.

What's that? No, I haven't got a job yet. In fact, I haven't started looking for work because I haven't figured out what I want to do.

Most days, I go to town and hang around with my friends there. My best friend Beyonce has got this crush on a Eurasian guy who works at HMV at the Heeren. So, mostly we go there and pester him to play our favourite CDs on the listening post. Beyonce is really havoc. While we listen through the headphones, she bops along to the songs and sings out snatches of lyrics to him, just to tease him.

Like that Alicia Keys' song, "Oooh... wooo... you don't know my name."

Eventually, he got the message and asked her for her name. He said his name was Conrad. He asked for my name too. I told him, even though he was not my type. He wore a ski cap and had a little goatee — US hip-hop style.

He also had on limited edition Adidas shoes and, fortunately, not too much bling (jewellery). Just a small gold cross around his neck. After all, he was just a salesman, right?

I could tell Beyonce and him belonged together. They both used the exact same handphone model and ringtone as well! It was fated.

Although I was happy for her, I felt like a lamp-post. Conrad was really sweet though. When we three went out together, he talked to me as well so I wouldn't feel left out.

And then, one Thursday afternoon, as all three of us were walking around Takashimaya during his tea break, I saw this beautiful black crocodile skin wallet that I really, really liked.

It cost $490, but for just that day, it was on sale for $89.90.

I showed it to them and they said it was nice too. But we didn't have $50 between the three of us. And so, well… you know, lah.

I pretended to put it back, then I slipped off its price tag, and pulled out the magnetic card with the bar code. Then, I coolly slipped it into my duffel bag.

But when I tried to walk out the door…

"Whee — wu — wheee-wu — wheee!!!"

The siren blared with red lights flashing. I was shocked. What could it be? I had removed the security barcode already! And when I saw Conrad and Beyonce walking away very quickly, I knew they had stolen something else as well.

And then I started to run.

We all met back at the Heeren where he carried on with his afternoon shift.

"Look what I got! I 'stunt' this just now!" said Beyonce, showing me this stupid, cheap plastic lanyard she had stolen. It cost only $4.90 — and it could have got all of us arrested!

I was so angry with her, I didn't say a word.

I avoided the lovey-dovey pair over the next few days. Really, that stupid Beyonce!

She called me a few times on the phone but I kept our conversations short.

All she talked about was Conrad, Conrad, Conrad. I mean, who cares, right?

Imagine my surprise when I got a call from him late one night just as I was about to turn my handphone off.

"Hello… Lauryn?! Guess who?"

It was a guy. Although I knew who it was, I pretended that I did not.

"Who's that?"

"It's Conrad."

"How did you get my number?" I said, trying to sound angry. But I wasn't.

"You know, Lauryn, I'm thinking of breaking up with Beyonce…" he said.

He was trying to sound sad but I could tell he wasn't.

"Because..." he sighed, and then, "Hold on, I have another call. Hello, Beyonce?"

My heart sank. And then "Hello, Lauryn? Yeah, it's me again…"

And then, he started telling me all kinds of things about Beyonce. I told him to stop. I so kay-poh, meh? Why would I want to know?

"Errr, Lauryn? My handphone battery is running flat. Want to meet me downstairs and talk? I am just below your block."

"Okay."

Of course, I didn't just go down to gossip about Beyonce. Conrad told me a lot about himself too.

The very next day, Beyonce called me to talk about Conrad. I tried to counsel her for I thought she'd be heartbroken. But she sounded very angry and bitter instead.

"By the way," she said. "He's not 24 like he said, you know? More like 30 years old already! I saw his IC."

"Really?" I said. But I didn't believe her.

"Also, did he try to show off that photo of his ex-girlfriend?" she asked.

I remember seeing the stunning photo he showed me.

"That's NOT his ex… it's Aishwarya Rai. A famous actress!"

"If she's so famous, why haven't I heard of her?"

"What? How come you so stupid all of a sudden? Har?"

" YOU'RE the stupid one."

"You… stupid… STOOOPIT …"

"STOOOPIT YOURSELF!"

I cut her off. I was expecting a call. But, hey, I'm not stupid okay?

I'm not in love with him or anythiing. Just curious and bored.

When I saw him again, I realised he DID look closer to 34 than 24. But still, he was pretty good looking for an older guy. What's more, he had made plans to go to a party on Friday.

"Many celebrities will be there!" he said, looking at me to see if I was impressed. I wasn't even trying to look impressed.

On Friday, I got all glammed up. Not for Conrad or his "celebrity" party. I dressed up to celebrate myself.

"Wow!" he said, when he came to pick me up on his motorbike. I strapped on the helmet with a shudder, thinking how it was flattening my hairdo.

"Ever tried E?" he asked.

"No," I said.

He handed me a pill and I popped it. It wasn't an E though. Just an ordinary sleeping pill.

"Let's Par-TAY!" he said, kick-starting the engine. I told him to go faster but he said he wasn't used to the bike. It was his friend's.

We wound our way through heavy traffic slowed down by a light drizzle, until we got to the "celebrity" party location.

It was a swank townhouse somewhere in District 10. There was a swimming pool that reflected the gloomy starless night.

The house itself was dark and silent, it didn't look like there was going to be a party. Conrad started "shucking" and "jiving", pulling the hood of his Kagol up after he took off his helmet.

"Yo, whaasup, DAWG!"

"My man, chilling out! Just chilling."

Conrad exchanged greetings with two of his colleagues from work. They acted as if they hadn't seen each other in years.

The only other people there were this couple and an old guy about my father's age. They were dressed casual in baggy shorts and slippers. And they just stared at my clothes and make-up.

"Well, Alvin, I guess we'd better get going," the couple said and left. The old guy, probably the owner of the house, was sweating all through his flimsy Hard Rock Cafe, New Zealand, tee-shirt.

Although he had flabby arms, he rolled up the short sleeves high and tight so his armpit hair poked out.

"A, check out some grooves man," someone said and started blasting the stereo up high.

"Turn it down," Alvin said and they turned it down immediately.

"Lauryn, this is Alvin, our store manager," said Conrad. "A wild and crazy guy… he's… mad!"

"So, Lauryn, is it?" said Alvin. "Want a drink?"

He gave me a beer and I drank it.

"Do you want another hit of Ecstasy?"

"I am ecstastic already."

Conrad and his two colleagues started shucking and jiving as if they were "high".

"Lauryn, ah? Lauryn, is it? Want another beer? How about… he he he… trying a cocktail with me?"

I looked the old jerk hard in the eyes. He

started shucking and jiving as well.

"Whaassup, Dawg?!"

"Yo, my man. Chill… chill out."

"Oh yah… uh huh… uh huh."

I looked at them. One Eurasian, one Malay, one Indian, one old Chinaman… all pretending to be American hip-hop blacks. It was like some new kind of racial harmony.

Alvin started drinking a lot of beer.

"Er… Lauryn, ah… I heard… I heard Conrad say you very sporting that type, is it?"

"I want to go home."

"Yo, BITCH, answer my man when he be talkin' to you, check?"

I asked Conrad to take me home.

"Err… okay, I'll send you back."

Alvin persisted. "Lauryn, is it? You got a contact number? Maybe I can call you."

"Thanks for the party, Uncle."

That made him shut up.

It started to rain heavily. I don't know how many pills and beer he had, but Conrad's motorbike started to sway recklessly on the wet, slick road. I put on my dark glasses and thought of Faye Wong in *Chungking Express*.

I didn't know what hit us.

I awoke, 24 hours later, on my back in the dark, within the safe medicinal smells of a hospital. A soft murmur of activity surrounded me.

With a sinking feeling, I knew from the sounds that it was daytime. But this darkness.

"I can't SEE… I CAN'T SEE… MY EYES!!! WHAT's happened to my EYES????" I screamed and screamed until they sedated me.

I awoke due to the dryness in my throat. The silence of a hospital at night was deafening.

I opened my eyes to a deeper darkness. I still couldn't see. I began to weep.

"Lauryn, don't cry…"

I was glad to hear Conrad's voice.

"Conrad, Conrad? Where are you?"

"I'm just here."

"My eyes! What happened to my eyes?"

" I'm sorry… I… I'm sorry…"

He was all choked up and crying. His remorse scared me more than anything. I began to wail.

"Shh… ssh… don't… don't… wait… maybe… maybe this will help… I got to go now."

"Huh?"

There was no reply. He was gone. But I felt the cold touch of his gold crucifix in my hand. It felt light and weightless. It probably wasn't even real gold. I lost conciousness again.

"Sis… sis…"

I heard my brother's voice, and another brother's wet snotty snivelling. And then, even before I could open my eyes, I could hear my parents nagging at me.

But I was glad to see them all. And I saw them before I realised I could SEE.

"Where's Conrad?"

"You can ask about that chup cheng kia some more!" my father scolded. But he changed his tone when my mother elbowed him in the ribs.

Then, she said, "He's… ker-chiang already. He died on the spot."

"But he can't have. He was here last night. I was just talking to him."

"Don't talk rubbish."

And then I remembered, and fell silent.

And when they saw Conrad's gold crucifix — with sunlight glinting off it — dangling from my wrist, they, too, fell silent.

My vision blurred again — this time from the tears I couldn't stop from flowing.

HOW TO SEE A GHOST

Derrick Ng, 12, student

I can see ghosts. It's a simple method which I'd like to share with your readers, Russell.

I heard that if you bend down and look back between your legs, you will be able to see something that you are not supposed to see, especially if it's done during the Lunar seventh month.

During the last Hungry Ghost Festival, my mother warned my brother and I not to use vulgar language or urinate in public. She said that we would offend some ghosts if we did those things.

I obeyed her but I wanted to try bending over and looking through my outstretched legs — just for the thrill of it, just to see what would happen. So, one night, when my mother was praying to her ancestors, I tried it out.

I didn't really expect to see anything, to tell you the truth, but imagine my shock when I beheld my deceased grandfather eating the food prepared by my mum. He looked angry at being disturbed and stormed his way towards me.

I collapsed in fear.

When I woke up, I was in bed. I told my mother what had happened and she scolded me for being so naughty and so stupid for tempting the ghosts.

I finally know the meaning of "curiosity kills the cat". I advise readers not to try this unless they are ready to face the consequences.

Russell Lee: And are you ready to face the consequences if your method doesn't work?

MANCHESTER UNITED FOREVER

Priscilla Chew, 16, student

It began as an ordinary shopping trip along Orchard Road earlier this year. I was window shopping, looking for a birthday present for Colin, my 17-year-old cousin.

I had absolutely no idea what to get him. What did he like? I was racking my brains and staring blankly at all the shops when I saw a strange man smiling at me and then beckoning me to enter a nearby shop.

I was puzzled. Who was he and what did he want? He was a young man, in his early twenties, and wearing a faded red shirt and shorts that showed off a pair of long, muscular legs.

On the back of his shirt were seven letters spelling EDWARDS. His hairstyle, short at the back and sides, looked old-fashioned, belonging more to the 1950s era.

Built like a tank, he had deep set eyes, bushy eyebrows and carried deep frowns on his forehead. A deep laughter line ran down the left side of his face.

As I continued staring at him, I realised that he was... translucent! I could see right through him. I almost freaked out.

However, I sensed that he did not mean any harm. I then felt a strong force of attraction pulling me into the shop that he was urging me to enter.

It was the Manchester United Superstore.

I was puzzling over why he wanted me to come in when he beckoned me over again. He was standing beside a rack of Manchester United replica kits.

I was pulled towards the shirt rack. I really couldn't control my movements. I think he was controlling them!

He pointed at a particular shirt on the rack. Did he want me to buy that for my cousin? I assumed he did.

I picked it out and saw that it was a Number 18 shirt with SCHOLES emblazoned boldly on it. Why did this man want me to buy a Paul Scholes jersey?

The man just winked at me and pointed at the counter. In a daze, I found myself paying for the shirt. He then whispered, "Colin will be lucky."

I never saw him again.

On arriving home, I quickly put the shirt away with trembling hands.

Two days after the encounter, I happened to be in my parents' room doing a bit of spring-cleaning when some photos in an old magazine caught my eye. I looked closer and read the article that followed.

It was about the victims of the 1958 Manchester United air disaster in Munich. One of the men in the pictures bore an uncanny resemblance to the man who had summoned me into the Manchester United Superstore.

That player was Duncan Edwards, one of the fabulous Busby Babes who had died in the tragic crash.

I felt a shiver run down my spine.

I didn't really think about that incident again until Colin's birthday. When he opened my present, he was over the moon.

He said that he had always wanted to own a Scholes jersey and asked how I knew that the ginger-haired midfielder was his favourite player.

I just shrugged my shoulders because I knew that no one would believe my story.

I was amazed about the solidarity of the Manchester United family. To think that a former great would care about a young fan so many miles and generations away.

But the story doesn't end there. Colin plays for his school team as a midfielder and he tells me that whenever he wears my present underneath his school jersey, his team always wins.

Colin says that his coach frequently singles him out for praise nowadays. Maybe Duncan Edwards has taken Colin under his protective wings.

Hopefully, I had played a part in launching Colin towards a great future in soccer...

A SPECIAL STORY

Russell Lee: Singapore's historic Bidadari Cemetery is a vast tract of land sprawling between Upper Serangoon and Upper Aljunied Roads. It contains graves that date back to the 19th Century. Now, all the graves are being exhumed so that a new housing development can occupy this valuable land. Work commenced in 2002 and is expected to be completed by 2006. But with the passing of Bidadari, I predict that thousands of new ghosts will be released, spirits who have lost their places of rest and have nowhere else to go but to roam the island...

THE LITTLEST ANGEL

Charles Ong, 49, teacher and photographer

As a keen photographer, I have spent many hours exploring Bidadari Cemetery. The beautifully-carved headstones offer many opportunities for black and white photography, which best captures the grim texture of the stonework as well as the subtle light and mood of the place.

Of all the hundreds of tombs and gravestones that I have shot, one stands out in my mind.

I discovered it one morning almost by accident — a tall, graciously carved, monumental headstone, with an angel mounted atop. At first I noticed nothing extraordinary. But on closer inspection, I was stunned to see that the little angel had a Chinese face.

My curiosity was immediately aroused and I began my research. It was the grave of a woman who died at the age of 28 in the early years of the 20th Century. The family had been wealthy Chinese merchants who had converted to Christianity. It appears that the woman died when her youngest son was only five. He was a cripple and, in those far off days, there was little medical science could do to help him. The bond between mother and son had been very close.

The heartbroken father was faced with the task of breaking the news to his little boy. "Your mother has gone to a nice place called Heaven," he consoled the weeping child.

The little boy looked up at his father and said with fierce determination, "Then I want to be an angel in Heaven and look after her."

The child was adamant and the anguished father feared for his son's will to live.

The father prayed for guidance and upon receiving his answer, went to the most renowned Chinese stonemason of the day and asked him to carve an angel for his wife's monument — an angel that was the exact likeness of his grieving son!

This the stonemason did and the small angelic figure mirrored the crippled boy.

When the boy attended the memorial service, he wept with joy when he saw his statue guarding his mother's grave.

Within a few years, however, weakened by his

physical condition, the young boy succumbed to influenza and died. The father, of course, buried his only son with his wife.

History does not record the father's fate and we can only hope that he was spared further pain in his life.

I pray that the littlest angel will not vanish from amongst us. I'm quite sure that the poor woman and her son would wish to be together eternally in stone, as they must surely be in some better place.

GHOST MARRIAGE

Polin Gumbek, 39, production controller

I'm sure that many have heard of "ghost marriages" where two people get involved in a marriage of convenience.

Usually, one marries to get citizenship in a particular country while the other gets paid a sum of money for their trouble.

But, Russell, have you ever heard of a human being marrying a ghost?

There are no witnesses to the wedding, no wedding photos, no wedding dinner and no marriage certificate to prove that it actually took place.

But it does happen.

This marriage happened 50 years ago in a very remote village in Sarawak, East Malaysia.

My grandmother was married to a ghost or the orang bunian. They were married long before I was born. The match was made by her superstitious parents.

My grandmother was happy enough with the arrangement though.

She gracefully led a double life, one in the real world and another with her invisible husband. I do not have any idea how my "grandfather" looked like. I guess nobody did except my grandma.

She led a normal life except for some unusual practices. There was a special loft constructed near the ceiling for her "husband".

Her mattress was directly below my grandfather's bedroom. His room consisted of a bed made of wood, coconut leaves, ripe coconuts, a sengkuang mat, twigs, clothes and various types of leaves.

There was no way I'd be alone in the house because I could always feel a ghostly presence.

Occasionally, she would put some food in a plate and leave it at the corner of his bedroom. My grandmother used to warn me that if I ever disturbed or ate the food, I would have a terrible stomachache.

Did you know that ghosts can suffer from lovesickness?

My grandpa was obviously very devoted to my grandmother. He couldn't stand to be apart from her.

My grandmother would always fall ill if she spent her nights elsewhere. But she would always recover once she returned home.

Once she spent three nights at my aunt's

place and developed a very high fever. My whole family was worried but she simply replied that her husband was missing her.

She rushed home, fed her husband and the fever came down immediately.

It remains a secret how she talked to her husband. Sometimes, when I went to her house to deliver some food, I could hear a conversation.

But I could never understand what she was saying. It was in some special tongue.

She didn't have any children during her marriage. She opted to adopt my mum and aunt.

How I hoped to see the progeny of a human-and-ghost marriage. Maybe my grandmother does have a child but in the form of a ghost!

Only my grandmother has the answer but she has brought it with her to her grave.

She died 25 years ago and her house has been vacant since. With no one to care for it, it has deteriorated. No one has had the courage to repair or demolish the house as it is believed to have an invisible undertaker.

As for myself, I firmly believe in the tradition of human marriage. But I admire my grandmother for her steadfast love to a ghost whom she was betrothed to so many years ago.

Unlike many marriages that break down, my grandmother truly fulfilled the vow of "till death do us part".

Russell Lee: Well, maybe they are not apart at all now...

PART IV

RUSSELL LEE INTERVIEWS MAIA LEE

Maia Lee is a firebrand of a performer who simply sizzles on stage. The Singapore Idol finalist is now a household name. This rock chick graced the May 2005 cover of FHM and was voted number eight in FHM Singapore's World's Most Sexiest Women list. Her debut English solo album, titled Maia — Emotionally Advised, was released on August 20, 2005.

MY UNWANTED GIFT

Maia Lee, 22, singer

Russell Lee: Thanks for taking time out from your busy schedule to meet us.

Maia: I'll always make time for one of my favourite authors.

Russell Lee: You are one of my favourite entertainers as well. I must have cast hundreds of votes for you during Singapore Idol.

Maia: Thank you for your support. You must check out my new album as well, okay?

Russell Lee: I was one of the first to get it. Now, I'm dying to hear your story.

I first discovered that I had "the third eye" when I was five. I've the ability to see spirits and other paranormal activities. It's not something I asked for. In fact, I wish I didn't have this "gift".

While growing up, people found me to be a disturbed kid because of the ability that I had.

I come from a family of Buddhists and we have a three-tiered altar in the living room.

It all started one night when I woke up around 2 am in the morning. I heard a "tok tok tok" sound coming from the living room and I looked out.

I saw that the statue of Buddha had levitated off the altar! We had another statue of a four-faced Buddha and his head was spinning around!

How could a bronze statue's head be spinning 360 degrees around and around?

Another statue of Kumanthong was expanding and deflating. The same was happening with the statue of Kuan Yin.

There were other figures running around on the altar and the scene just freaked me out. I couldn't stop crying.

Eventually, I fell asleep. That was when I knew I had the third eye as I began seeing "things" on a frequent basis.

I would also have premonitions and my dreams would come true. When I was young, my mum realised I had a special gift and would ask me for 4D numbers.

If I was in the mood to tell her, the numbers would frequently be correct. That is about the only bright side of having the third eye.

I have seen so many supernatural things that it is almost second nature to me.

One of the most scary incidents I have encountered was when I went on a trip to Chengde and Beijing with the Ngee Ann Secondary School orchestra.

This was when I was in Secondary Two. We checked into the Yunshan (Cloud Mountain) Motel in Chengde and I immediately felt that the building was "dirty".

Normally, I don't see faces but I had a good look in China. I was assigned Room 808 and the door was facing the staircase.

In geomancy, it is not good luck to have a door facing the staircase.

When I went to my room, I saw one ghostly being sitting at the staircase and there were three others along the corridor.

It did not help that the hotel lighting was green. It made the scene all the more spookier.

Later in the lobby, I met a male teacher who was a Taoist. He, too, sensed that something was amiss.

We took a lift up together and the lift stopped on the fifth floor. We saw an old man and an old woman standing outside.

They had white hair and we could see right through them. My teacher was scared out of his wits while I was relatively calm.

He kept pressing the button for the lift door to close and his whole body was shaking. After what seemed an eternity, the door finally closed.

I thought that being an elder, he should have been less afraid. However, his face was pale and his legs were wobbly as he alighted on the seventh floor while I got out on the eighth.

Things were okay when we returned to Beijing.

FIRE HAZARD

I was working with a mobile phone company in 2002 before I joined the Music and Drama Company.

I was with the front line staff. One Sunday afternoon, I was resting at my desk when I saw a figure approaching.

The man looked like he had been badly burnt and patches of skin were hanging from his face. His skin looked as if someone had just thrown acid at him.

I quickly grabbed my things and went home, saying that I was not feeling well. But my colleagues could see that something had frightened the living daylights out of me.

The next day, my manager took me aside and asked me if I had seen something unnatural. I nodded my head.

He said that there had been a fire at the place where we were working and many people had been burnt to death, including a pregnant woman.

I wonder if it was one of these unfortunate spirits that I had encountered.

VIEW FROM MY ROOM

When I was in Secondary One, I had a disturbing view from my bedroom window.

Every other night, for four years, I would see two figures floating up and down. They appeared to be a woman and a young child, maybe two to three years old.

I asked my mother about them and she said that when I was very young, a young mother from the opposite block had leapt to her death with her child in her arms.

When I saw the figures, I felt more sad than scared. I would pray for their souls and that they would find rest.

LOSING MYSELF

In 2002, I went to watch a friend perform at Mad Monk's Bar in Boat Quay.

I reached there around 9 pm. The next thing I knew, I was outside lying on the ground next to the river.

There were lots of people and police surrounding me. Apparently, I had passed out.

I found out later that it was already midnight. Till today, I cannot account for those missing three hours.

My colleague later told me that I had apparently walked out, as if in a trance, and I kept pointing at the Riverwalk building saying, "You ren tiao lou, you ren tiao lou" or "someone is jumping down, someone is jumping down".

I have no recollection at all of what had happened. I did not touch any liquor so I could not possibly have been drunk.

Could I have been possessed?

THE YAMAHA ORGAN

When I was 19, I used to own a hand-me-down Yamaha organ. The previous owners gave it to me even though I barely knew them. I guess they knew I was into music.

One night when I was sleeping, I awoke suddenly but I couldn't move. I felt heavy and I could see my left foot being "pulled" by a strange force.

As I looked on, I could see my leg being stretched. To my horror, it was getting longer and longer.

My elongated leg seemed translucent.

The next thing I knew, I was sitting across from my bed looking at myself.

It definitely wasn't a dream. I was awake at that time. It's a feeling I can't describe — to actually be looking at yourself from across a room.

I shut my eyes and just prayed and prayed. Then I found myself back on my bed.

But it didn't end there. I was still immobilised. I heard the irritating, loud noise of moving furniture, and it was growing louder and louder.

From the corner of my eye, I saw the heavy organ chair moving across my room to my bedside. I yelled for my parents and when they came into the room, I could finally get up, and the chair was back in its original position. I ended up sleeping with my parents that night.

The next day, we disposed of the organ and the chair that came with it.

NAKED MAN OF BLOCK 107

This was one of my more interesting experiences.

I had just knocked off from work and I was going back to my home in Bedok North.

I was walking along the corridor when I saw a figure running towards me at full speed.

It was very tall — maybe 1.9 to 2 metres tall — which is very unusual. It was also very skinny... and naked.

The most unusual thing was that this figure was levitating about 1.2 metres above the ground as it ran.

His skin looked very tanned. I could not tell if he was Malay or Chinese.

When I reached home, I had a stunned expression on my face. My father, who was used to seeing me in this state, knew that something had happened.

All he said was, "Qu chong liang, shui jiao" or "Go take a shower and go to sleep."

A few months later, I saw this figure again. I dubbed him "The Naked Man of Block 107".

I can laugh about such things now but believe me, they aren't funny at the time.

For a long time, I was scared out of my wits

and you would not catch me talking about such things as I do now.

CLOSING THE THIRD EYE

I have so many stories to tell that they can probably fill up your entire book, Russell.

I have seen the ghosts of accident victims while on board a taxi, decomposing corpses walking around and I have even seen an all-white figure floating around in my recording studio.

I guess I've grown used to such things.

The point I'm trying to make is that spirits do not wander around only during the Seventh Month. They are around every moment of the day.

About two years ago, I went for an elaborate ritual at a temple to "gai yan" or "close the eye". The master told me to keep the ceremony a secret.

Since then, things have improved. But this unwanted gift of mine still keeps presenting itself from time to time.

Russell Lee: Thank you for sharing your experiences with us Maia. Best of luck in your career.

Maia: Thank you. It's been a pleasure.

RUSSELL LEE INTERVIEWS WINONA WEE

Winona Wee is a precocious young talent on the child modelling scene. This Primary Five student at CHIJ (Kellock) has appeared in TV advertisements for Nickelodeon. She has also featured in a documentary, touting the virtues of drinking milk, which is making the rounds in primary schools. Besides modelling, she enjoys playing netball, surfing the Internet and reading.

MY NEW FRIEND

Russell Lee: How are you, my young friend?

Winona: Hi, Russell. I'm fine except that I'm a little nervous meeting you face to face.

Russell Lee: Relax, I'm very friendly despite appearances.

Winona: I'm just such a big fan of yours. It's a thrill to meet you and talk to you. I had met you before during one of your storytelling sessions on stage at Singapore Expo.

Russell Lee: I'm just as happy to meet you, Winona. I hear you have an interesting story for us. I hand the stage over to you. Showtime.

Winona: Well, this story took place at the end of August, 2005. I went with a group of friends to catch a movie at a cineplex in town.

79

It was a Saturday afternoon and we had arranged to meet at 12 pm. We bought tickets for the 2 pm show of *The Maid,* then we went for lunch.

We decided to have Kentucky Fried Chicken. Since we were going to watch a horror movie, the topic of our conversation naturally gravitated towards the supernatural.

"Do you guys know that one of the cinema halls here is haunted?" said Petrina, one of my friends.

I was taken aback but, apparently, a few other friends had heard the story before.

For my benefit, Petrina told me what she knew about the resident ghost of the cinema.

Apparently, the ghost of a little girl loved to watch movies too and had been spotted sitting in the front row of Halls 2 and 4 in this particular cineplex. She seemed to prefer the first and last shows of the day.

Petrina said she had read many stories about this little girl on the Internet. It seems that the cleaners would find toys lying around after the last show. If they left these toys by the exit at the end of the night, they would be gone the next morning.

But they would magically reappear in the front seats after the last show that night!

A few patrons had even reported seeing a little girl — hugging some soft toys — watching movies on her own. But when the lights came on, the little girl was nowhere to be seen.

This story made my hair stand on ends! I was fascinated by it. I kept asking Petrina and my friends for more details but they were very sketchy.

"Oh, I hope that I will have a chance to see this little girl later," I wished silently.

It then occurred to me to check which hall we would be watching the show in. My friends let out an audible sigh of disappointment (or was it relief?) when we saw that we would be going to Hall 3 instead.

"Who knows? We might find her during our show as well," said another friend, Bee Ean.

After lunch, we did some window-shopping before making our way to the cinema. I bought some buttered sweet corn and a Coke and we made our way into the cinema.

My friends had already forgotten about our earlier conversation and they seemed oblivious to the fact that they were in a hall where there could be one non-paying customer. They were just eagerly waiting for the show to start.

We were about six rows from the front and I scanned the seats in front of me eagerly, hoping to catch a glimpse of a little girl clutching her soft toys. I was mildly disappointed when I saw that the first row was empty. There was no sign of her.

"It's just a story, silly," I thought to myself. "Besides, we're not even in the right hall."

I settled back and waited for the show to start. A young couple, in their early 20s, occupied the seats in front of us. They were accompanied by a cute little boy, who was about six years old.

"Wow, they seem pretty young to be parents," I thought. "But maybe the little boy is the younger brother of one of them."

The show started and I was soon engrossed by the plot. Every so often, I was distracted by the little boy who would pop his head over the seat and point a little toy gun at me.

I just smiled each time. "He's too young to enjoy the show," I thought.

Towards the end of the movie, I heard something drop. It bounced around and hit my leg. I bent down to pick it up and saw that it was a marble.

"It must be the little boy's," I thought.

Not wanting to bother the people in front as the show was nearing its climax, I put the marble in my pocket.

When the show finally ended, everyone started to make their way to the exits.

I stood up and looked for the little boy to return his marble. But he was nowhere to be found.

Thinking that he had gone to the toilet, I tapped the young man on his shoulder. "Excuse me, I think this belongs to the little boy who was with you," I said.

"What do you mean?" he said. "There was no one beside me except my girlfriend."

I felt goosebumps. How could that be? The couple then made their way to the exit.

My friends asked me what I was holding in my hand and I showed it to them.

"How did you get the marble?" Petrina asked.

I told them the story of the little boy. "Come on, you guys," I said. "Surely you must have seen him. He was pointing the gun at us so many times during the show!"

My friends were all flabbergasted. They were all sure that the couple didn't have any company.

"I'm very sure because I took a good look at them as they came in," said Bee Ean. "I thought the guy looked quite cute."

I was really perplexed now. I left the marble on the floor and quickly walked out of the cinema.

My friends were quite spooked as well.

We have since discussed this incident many times in school. Maybe this little boy is the brother of that little girl and they wander around different halls before meeting up at the end of the day.

Russell Lee: Thanks for sharing that story, Winona. As I like watching movies myself, I'll be looking out for these two little kids.

Winona: I should have kept the marble to show you, Russell.

Russell Lee: I'll try and confirm these sightings soon. In the meantime, take care and study hard.

Winona: Thanks, Russell. I'll take you along the next time I go to the cinema, okay?

PART V

A SPECIAL STORY

THE JEALOUS GHOST

Suzanne Yeo, 26, kindergarten teacher

Hi, Russell. This is my first time writing in even though I have all your books. I used to wonder whether the stories in your books were true and whether ghosts really existed.

Those doubts were dispelled when I met one a few months ago!

I was on cloud nine after a lovely night out with my boyfriend, Jason. He had taken me for a romantic candlelit dinner at Pasir Panjang Village and we cuddled up after dinner on a park bench, taking in the view at Mount Faber and enjoying each other's company.

Jason is my knight in shining armour. He is caring, considerate and, best of all, he listens to me — unlike my ex, Tommy, who was a chauvinistic pig.

After Tommy, I was reluctant to risk being hurt again. But Jason, whom I met at a friend's wedding, helped me regain my trust in men and I finally dared to love again.

We started off as friends and this slowly deepened into a mutual fondness for each other. We began going steady and, after a year, I finally felt that I had found someone I could spend the rest of my life with.

Jason is not a glib talker and while it may be easy for some men to shower women with gifts and flowers, the thing that matters to every woman is sincerity. That's what I think anyway.

What I love about him is that he gives me his full attention and does not ogle every sweet young thing that passes by. I feel secure in his presence.

When I got home that night, it was close to midnight and I took a shower before getting ready to settle into bed. I turned on the radio, expecting to be greeted by my favourite love songs on Gold 90.5FM.

Instead of a soothing ballad greeting my ears, I was puzzled when unfamiliar strains of a Chinese opera greeted my ears.

"Has someone been fiddling with my radio?" I thought to myself. My dial was always set on Gold.

Feeling slightly irritated, I went over to take a look at the radio. To my bewilderment, the digital display showed 90.5.

I made sure that I was in FM mode and not AM. Everything was in order yet the opera music was relentless. I fiddled with the radio and it was business as usual on the other stations. But when I returned to Gold, it was the same Chinese opera music on air.

Shrugging my shoulders, I slipped in an Air Supply CD. I absolutely went bonkers when the same monotonous strains of Chinese opera came out over the speakers. I screamed and ran to my parents' room. They were sleeping but my hysterical cries awoke them.

I was sobbing and crying and not coherent. They managed to calm me down enough for me to explain what had happened. They promptly accompanied me to my room only to hear Air Supply's "All Out of Love" from my stereo.

"Could it have been a bad dream, Suzanne?" my mother asked. I hadn't even fallen asleep so I couldn't have been dreaming. But I could offer no explanation.

I refused to sleep in my room that night and hauled my mattress and pillow over to my parents' room and slept on the floor instead.

I went to work as usual the next day and I called Jason during lunch to tell him what had happened. He was at a loss for words.

He picked me up from work and we had a subdued dinner before he sent me home. He stayed with me till midnight and there were no problems with my radio.

Was I going mad? Had I imagined it all? I decided not to burden Jason any further and asked him to go home. He reluctantly agreed.

I took my shower and got ready for bed. This time I did not try my luck with the radio. Instead, I left the lights on and tried to go to sleep.

Within a few minutes, I felt the room getting colder even though I had not switched on the air-conditioning.

I pulled the blanket over myself but wild thoughts were swimming through my mind. Suddenly, the light went out by itself and I felt a dark presence smothering me.

I wanted to scream but nothing left my lungs. I couldn't breathe properly and I felt as if someone was strangling me... suffocating me.

Then gradually, the grip loosened and I heard

a whisper. "I'm sorry for scaring you," a young woman's voice said. "I'm just so jealous that you have such a wonderful boyfriend."

I was paralysed with fear and couldn't summon myself to run to my parents' room. I just lay there trembling under the covers.

"My name is Siew Lee," the voice continued. "I am a lonely ghost. I was never attractive when I was young and no boys fancied me. I died a lonely spinster."

"But what... what... has that got to do with me?" I stammered.

"I used to live in this block and I roam around here all the time," the voice said. "I've noticed how loving you and your boyfriend are and I followed you home last night.

"When I saw how happy you were, I decided to play a prank on you. I won't do it again, I promise."

With that, the lights came on again and the sense of eeriness left the room.

I took a huge gulp of air as I tried to make sense of it all. In a way, I felt sad for Siew Lee.

Since then, there have been no problems with my stereo. Jason and I are now engaged to be married. In my heart of hearts, I will be throwing the bridal bouquet just for Siew Lee in the hope that she will find peace and comfort.

A MOTHER'S LOVE

Joseph Lee, 10, student

Russell, I don't know whether you will believe me or not. I'm going to share a real story about my mother and me.

My mother was still alive three years ago. She taught me about life and loved me very much. We were very close.

She worked for a major department store in Singapore, and she must have been doing well because they sent her to Paris to work for one week. When she told me she was coming home, I was very happy because I had missed her so much.

But something unexpected happened on the plane. She had a headache and died on board. I couldn't believe it. She had been so healthy and it was so sudden.

I was so sad I cried for many days — every time I thought about her, my tears would flow. It was tough having to go back to school after the funeral because my heart was still heavy and I was hurting.

When I came back from school, I saw a cake on the table. I thought it was my aunt who had bought it, so I ate it. When I saw a cake again the next day after returning from school, I began to suspect that it might not have been from my aunt after all.

On the third day, I attended a school camp and had to stay outdoors. I saw a cake again — this time it was placed on top of my sleeping bag just before I was about to tuck myself in.

I knew it couldn't have been my aunt because she must have been in bed at that time. And she wouldn't have bothered to make the long journey just to give me some cake.

Only my mother knew that I loved to eat cakes. She would buy me cakes all the time when she was alive. I had a strange feeling that it was my mother who had sent me the cakes.

After the camp, I went to the graveyard to pray to my mother.

"Mother, don't worry," I told her. "I will take good care of myself."

From that day, I never received anymore cakes. I think my mother was finally able to rest in peace.

ARMY DAZE

Ricky Lee, 39, art director

Hi, Russell. How are you doing? My son brought home a copy of *TSGS 12* recently. I told him that I had a ghost story of my own to tell and he asked me to share it with you after he heard it.

I studied advertising in Miami and I returned home to do my National Service after graduation in 1987. I enjoyed my stay in the United States as I loved driving around the country with my girl-friend, Ivy, and taking in the beautiful scenery.

The days were carefree, spent playing tennis, relaxing at the beach and having barbeques in the backyard while drinking beer.

Ivy was a Malaysian girl who was born in Penang but had studied in Singapore. She was my first love. I had never held a girl's hand until I met her and, of course, I shared my first kiss with her.

We had been going steady for 10 months before I had to return to Singapore. However, she still had 18 months to go before she completed her accountancy course.

So, it was with mixed feelings that I returned home. I was glad that I had successfully completed my course and to be reunited with my family again. But I missed Ivy dearly.

It did not help that I had to report for my Basic Military Training (BMT) two weeks after I returned home. Not knowing what to expect, I reported to the old Central Manpower Base. We were bundled into three-tonners and sent off to Pulau Tekong.

I was in the Polytechnic batch and the guys were cool. I made a lot of good friends during BMT. The training was hell though, especially since I was out of shape. Ivy was a good cook and I had put on a lot of weight.

I was within a few body fat percentage points of being put in the obese platoon. Eventually, I was made a part of Bravo Company in Camp One.

There were a few shocks in store. I almost couldn't recognise myself in the mirror after a Malay barber shaved off my hair.

There were a few barbers at work and by the time they had finished, there was a big pile of hair on the floor.

The plus point was that there was no need to

comb my hair and being in the hot sun, having a botak head helped keep us cool.

The first few weeks were hell. We had to go for long runs and training exercises in the jungle. The arms drills were complicated and I always seemed to mess up whatever I was doing.

I was given the nickname "sotong" for being so muddle-headed. I was always "blur like sotong".

Once, I even left the firing pin of my M16 in the parade ground after re-assembly. Fortunately, my platoon mates helped me to find it. The thought of being charged terrified me.

I had a sadistic corporal, named Razali, who delighted in terrorising us. Push-ups, change parades (where you have to change from uniform to PT kit and back again) and endless drills under the scorching sun in the parade square were standard punishments.

Crawling around as part of the butt party during live-firing exercises was something which this corporal made us do.

I missed the free and easy times I had back in the States. Days were spent thinking of Ivy and nights were spent looking at her pictures.

Pulau Tekong was rumoured to be haunted but I never believed much in ghosts. However, without my knowledge, my platoon mates were being terrified and all of them blamed me for it.

"It's all your fault," said my buddy Chee Hong. "You are the only one who came back from the States. You must have brought an American ghost back with you."

Apparently, many of my platoon mates had

heard voices in the toilet. Many were now afraid to go in after dark.

"But I haven't heard anything," I said. "And how do you know he's an American ghost?"

"Because he speaks with an American accent," said Chee Hong. "I sometimes have trouble understanding what he's saying. I just run out from the toilet."

This "American ghost" was fast becoming the talk of the platoon. About 10 had already heard his voice while the rest were mystified.

There was even one recruit who asked to be transferred to Camp Two because of this.

Those who had heard voices all concurred that it was a foreign accent. The weirdest thing was that this ghost kept saying things like "Where are the girls?" or "Show me the girls".

Well, he certainly wouldn't find many in Pulau Tekong.

And definitely not in our toilet.

The bravest guy in our platoon, Davinder, finally summoned the courage to talk to the ghost when he heard the voice again one night.

According to Davinder, he had asked the spirit what he was doing there.

"I haven't been lucky in love," the ghost said. "I want a nice Asian woman who is gentle and caring. Just like Ricky's girlfriend."

So it was true. The ghost had followed me home to Singapore after all.

Strangely, I never got to hear his voice. But, over time, those who did meet him found him to be harmless. One wise guy even named him the

"Sarong Party Ghost".

We didn't know how to help the ghost until Teck Wei suggested that we take him to Choa Chu Kang Cemetery.

Maybe the American ghost would get lucky there.

After all, there would be a host of spirits at Choa Chu Kang, right?

So we wrote a note on the toilet wall telling the ghost to follow us when we booked out on Friday night.

We added, of course, that he was not to bother any of us at home.

Instead of going to a tea dance like we usually did on Saturdays, a group of us met up and went to Choa Chu Kang Cemetery.

We were not sure whether "he" was with us but we kept telling him that he should hang out there instead of at Pulau Tekong. His chances of finding "a girl" would be much higher.

We eventually went back to camp and never heard any voices again until the night before our passing-out parade.

A few guys were startled initially when a happy-sounding voice rung out, "Thanks guys, without your help I wouldn't have met May!"

Eventually, we all had a good chuckle about it.

Unfortunately, things with Ivy did not work out and I eventually married someone else.

I sometimes still wonder about the extra member of our platoon: Is he still with May or has he moved on to "fresher blood"?

CHARM SOUP FOR A YOUNG MAN

Mabel, 45, school principal

I was born and raised in a remote village in Kudat, Sabah. In 1977, I had to move to Kota Kinabalu to continue my Form Six.

I stayed with my aunt who was a "working girl", a sex worker, when she was young. She lived with different men until she was 40.

Then she retired and moved in with an old man who owned a garage.

One day, she fell into a trance while she was crossing the road. She just stood in the middle of the road like a statue. A male medium noticed her and dragged her away from an oncoming car.

They became close friends. He taught her black magic and helped her set up a big altar in her house. She offered food regularly to three deities and made sure that the joss sticks were smouldering all the time.

I believe that the medium taught her black magic on how to retain her youth. And how to capture someone's heart.

This is because she took the 18-year-old son of the garage owner as her toy boy after the old man died.

How she managed to attract him baffled me. She was an overweight woman with heavy jowls, a big belly and fat hips.

On the other hand, he was a rather good-looking young man with an unassuming manner.

After a tiring day at the garage, he would

head straight into the bathroom where she would scrub him clean.

I could hear them laughing and fooling around in the bathroom every evening.

But she was very insecure. One afternoon, she started screaming at me and told me to leave her "husband" alone.

She swore that she had seen me hugging and kissing him in the morning even though I was innocent. She said that "a piece of paper can never cover up a fire" and that "a chick will eventually come out of its shell".

It was all too "cheem" or complex for me. Eventually, I figured out she was implying that I was hiding something. She even challenged me to kneel in front of the altar to prove my innocence.

I was so shocked and frightened by her baseless accusations that I rushed out of the house, never to return again.

In 1982, I went to the United States to continue my studies. When I returned home 10 years later, my cousin told me that my aunt was still living with the same young man.

I was astounded as she had to be at least 55 while he was just 33 (these were the days before older woman-younger man, Demi Moore-Ashton Kutcher-type relationships were hip!). Surely, he could do better than stay with an old hag.

That was in 1992. The last I heard of them was in 2004 when my cousin attended their only daughter's wedding.

My cousin remarked that my aunt and her live-in lover didn't look a day older than the day they first met in 1977.

She must have found the secret to prolonging her youth.

I looked at a picture taken at the wedding and saw that my aunt had not aged even though she was still as fat as ever.

My cousin said that she once saw my aunt burning a piece of yellow paper, with mystical writing on it, in the kitchen.

She let the ashes fall into a bowl of soup. She drank from the bowl and served the rest to our "uncle".

That must be the reason why she had been able to mesmerise him for so long. I bet the talisman is their fountain of youth and everlasting love.

How an ugly, old ex-hooker could hold a young man's heart for so long is mind-boggling. I wonder how often she has to serve her "charm soup" to keep him from straying.

After all, he is only 46 while she is almost 70!

VALE OF TEMPE

Eric Tan, 19, student

In Penang, Malaysia, there is an infamous road called the Vale of Tempe.

The road was built more than a hundred years ago to provide access to a reservoir. Just under two kilometres, it cuts across a hill joining two suburbs. The reservoir entrance is situated somewhere in the middle of the narrow and winding road. Numerous mysterious accidents have happened along this stretch. Many victims have driven off a high cliff, and several other fatal accidents have also been reported.

Many Penangites, including myself, are afraid of using this road at night. It is rumoured to be haunted.

I did some research and found out that an innocent girl was once killed by a policeman along this road.

No one knows why. It was perhaps a case of mistaken identity. It is rumoured that the ghost of this girl now has a vendetta against every single policeman! So it's no surprise that policemen avoid this road, especially when night falls. Apparently, she will cause an accident to befall any policeman using the Vale of Tempe.

I'm not sure though if the ghost would do the same to a policewoman.

Another story explains the reason for the mysterious accidents at a cliff where many cars have swerved off. Locals say there was a fatal accident along that road a long time ago. A young lady had died instantly in that accident.

Her soul has not been able to rest in peace and she has been haunting the road since.

She will often appear late at night out of nowhere in front of an ill-fated driver. As the road is winding and very narrow, with the cliff on one side, many victims have perished trying to avoid her. From most accounts, she has long hair and wears a white gown.

Not long ago, my friend, Adrian, and I were

driving along the Vale of Tempe at around 1 am after a church meeting.

There were no other vehicles along the road at that time. Adrian was driving while I was in the passenger seat. Driving at a comfortable speed while taking the sharp curves along the winding road, we were approaching the gate to the reservoir when we saw a lady in white standing in the middle of the road.

Her back was to us and we could only see that she had long hair.

Adrian slowed down upon seeing her. I refused to believe that it was *the* ghost. It just felt strange that there would be a woman walking along this dark, secluded road at such a late hour.

As we drove closer, the lady slowly turned around and faced us. To our horror, we saw that her face was covered in blood!

Adrian was sure this was no human and gunned the accelerator, hoping to run through her and get away as fast as possible.

There didn't seem to be any impact when we drove right through her. I turned around to check if she was still there. Instead, I saw her head inside the car! Separated from its body, it was stuck between the rear window and the back seat, where the speakers and third brake lights usually are.

I was so scared I didn't know what to do or say. Adrian looked at the rear-view mirror and saw that the lady, now headless, was chasing after us. She wanted her head back!

He tried to drive away as fast as possible. The

winding and narrow road made it difficult but he tried his best.

Both of us said our prayers and hoped that the ordeal would be over soon.

Once we negotiated the winding bends, Adrian took another look at the rear-view mirror and saw that the ghost was no longer behind us.

He asked me to turn around to double-check. I confirmed that there was no one behind and to my great relief, I saw that the head had also disappeared from the car.

This is one experience I will never forget — I still wake up in sweat sometimes as she continues to haunt me in my sleep.

NAUGHTY BABY

Tony Wong, 30, engineer

I've heard many stories about Kampong Java Park, sitting next to Kandang Kerbau Hospital, being haunted. Then again, many other places in Singapore also have restless spirits lurking.

However, I'm convinced that this park has other inhabitants besides the turtles and fish in the lily pond.

When my wife was eight months' pregnant, I took her to KK Hospital for a routine check-up. After that, we went to the food court for dinner.

I suggested buying bread to feed the turtles and my wife agreed. We strolled to the park. My wife sat down on the bench while I fed the turtles.

Out of the corner of my eye, I saw a toddler

slowly walking towards the lily pond.

"Where are his parents?" I wanted to ask.

The toddler got dangerously close and I rushed to prevent him from falling in. However, I was too late. There was a little splash as he wandered over the edge. Without hesitation, I plunged in to save him. I quickly tried to put my arms around him — a cute Chinese boy, fair and plump. But he simply vanished into thin air and I found myself staring into empty space!

My wife walked over and asked what had happened. A few passers-by were also curious and asked if I needed help.

I climbed out and told them what had happened. My wife said that she had her eyes on me all the time and she had not seen any baby.

Neither did any of the passers-by.

It must have been a baby ghost with a sense of humour. I did some research on Kampong Java Park and found out that it was once a Jewish cemetery. Another source said it used to be a mass burial ground during World War II.

My wife and I are now the proud parents of our own bouncing baby boy. Nowadays when I want to relax, I take my family to the Botanic Gardens or MacRitchie Reservoir instead.

MY HOMESICK UNCLE

Amy Chiang, 46, accounts clerk

I'd like to tell you a story about my third uncle from my father's side.

In Hainanese, we call third uncle "ta teh". He died when I was in Secondary One.

I remember that night well. There was a knock on our door and when my mum opened it, there were two policemen standing outside.

My parents and I immediately knew that they were not there to bring good news. At first, we thought something bad had happened to one of my sisters or brother.

But they broke the news of my third uncle instead. Hainanese men are renowned as good cooks and sailors. My father and uncle loved the sea. My dad sailed around Southeast Asia while the world was my third uncle's oyster.

It was at Port Elizabeth in South Africa that my uncle was beaten to death. He had been trying to help a pregnant woman who was being robbed.

For his kindness, he was attacked by two men, robbed and killed. The worst part is that the pregnant woman was an accomplice.

According to South African police investigations, she was actually the bait and many passers-by had fallen into their trap.

Maybe it was fated. Just before my third uncle died, a fortune-teller had told my mother that he would not live past the age of 45.

And, Russell, he was 45 when he died. I was told that the Chinese believe that there are certain obstacles to clear when they reach a certain age.

In Hokkien, they say 45 is "pai woon" or bad luck.

My third uncle's spirit eventually made its

way back to Singapore, as my husband found out.

After my parents moved and stayed with my older brother in Tampines, I bought over the house from my parents.

I enjoyed a blissful time there with my husband until he started coming home late and sometimes not at all.

The usual shouting games and quarrels followed until my husband told me the reason.

He asked me whether I knew a tall, thin man and gave a detailed description. It sounded exactly like my third uncle.

My husband told me that he disliked coming home because he would have this bad headache every time he opened the gate.

Once, he felt a big whack on his head as he was opening the gate. When he turned around, he caught a glimpse of a tall, thin man floating away.

That is when I took out a photo of my third uncle and showed it to my husband. He said it was definitely my third uncle who had hit him.

When I told my mum what had happened, she went to consult a temple medium. We realised that when my parents had shifted home, we had forgotten to tell my third uncle during the usual prayer sessions.

You see, my mum makes it a point to pray and make offerings to my third uncle every year on his death anniversary.

Ta teh must have been wondering why there had been no offering this year and, upon seeing a stranger, must have whacked his head each time he came by.

The story ends happily though. The temple medium told my mum to make offerings and prayers along the corridor and to tell my third uncle to go to Tampines instead.

My husband doesn't come home late now. He had better not or I will be the one whacking his head!

NOT A TECHNICAL PROBLEM

Ian Ong, 20, national serviceman

Have you every been in a lift that stops at a level but there's nobody outside? Happens all the time, right?

What do you make of it? Pranksters? A technical problem? Well, I think I can explain. Believe it or not, there could be something which you and I cannot see entering the lift and standing next to you.

It all started with a freak motorbike accident that landed me in hospital for three weeks. According to the doctor, it was a miracle that I was able to survive after being flung down at more than 100 kilometres per hour.

Things started to go wrong a week after I gained consciousness. I began to see things which other people could not.

She was a little girl, around five years old, in a pink hospital gown. Holding on to a teddy bear, she stood outside the lift at Level 4 and looked at me with her big round eyes.

I was on crutches trying to get to the garden

when the lift stopped. I was waiting for the girl to come in when a nurse said, "Stop dreaming. There's nobody outside. Release the button."

"Can't you see the little girl?" I asked.

As I turned around, I realised the little girl was standing right behind me. I wondered why the nurse hadn't noticed her.

When I alighted at the ground floor, I tried to look for the little girl. But she was nowhere to be seen. I was baffled.

The lift did not make any other stops.

That night, I told my supervising doctor but he dismissed it as an illusion, saying that I had taken a bad knock to my head.

Maybe he was right since nothing happened for the next two weeks.

Then it started again during the last night of my hospital stay. Like the first time, this also involved the lift.

That night, I was going back to my ward alone after my physiotherapy session. I entered the lift on the second floor with a cleaner.

At the third storey, two white-haired elderly men stepped in. The lift stopped again at the fourth level. I held on to the button for a granny in a wheelchair to come in.

I got the shock of my life when I happened to glance at the side panel of the lift which was a mirror.

I saw that I was the only one in the lift!

I was scared stiff. I prayed that the lift would move faster but it seemed to be ascending at a snail's pace.

The air in the lift also seemed to get colder with each passing second. I shuddered. My heart kept pounding faster and faster.

When the lift finally reached the fifth floor, I walked out slowly, afraid that my trembling steps would betray me.

As I quickened my pace, I noticed the same little girl, whom I saw two weeks ago, standing along the corridor.

She smiled and waved at me.

That was the last straw! I hobbled back to the corridor as fast as my feet would take me and collapsed into my bed.

Somehow, I managed to fall asleep and was discharged the next day.

Nowadays, I try and avoid taking the lift whenever I can. But when I have no choice, I feel a cold and clammy sweat.

I don't know who I'll meet next.

THE GHOST OF NEWTON CIRCUS

Lai Poh Kit, 31, salesman

Russell, have you ever seen ghosts in a Singapore hawker centre? Most people will tell you they haven't, but I don't believe them.

There have been many murders in our hawker centres and coffee shops, especially in Geylang, and the spirits of the dead must still be present. I should know, Russell, because I once had contact with such a spirit.

Some friends and I had been out drinking one

night and by 2 am we were ready to call it a night. But because we were hungry, we took a cab to Newton Circus.

Over the years Newton Circus has witnessed its share of murders and assaults in the wee hours of the morning. Of course, when my friends and I went there, death was the last thing on our minds.

While my friends went in search of food, I looked for a table. It was crowded but I managed to find a table with only one occupant, over by some shadowy bushes in a corner. I went up to the man and asked him if my friends and I could share his table. He was Caucasian and I was not sure if he had more friends coming to join him.

He said we'd be welcome, but before I could even sit down I caught a look at his face in the dim light. It was streaked with blood, and one eye appeared to be missing. Russell, it was a very horrible sight!

The man sensed my fear and smiled. Then he told me his story.

He said he had been brutally beaten to death at this very table. He had been drunk at the time, and had made some insulting remarks to a group of Chinese drinkers close by. When his friends tried to make him leave, he refused and insisted on staying for one more drink. His friends, sensing how easily he could provoke a fight, begged him to return home with them. But no, he shouted, he could look after himself!

The minute his friends had left, the liquor started talking again. He hurled more abuse at the locals and they responded. The insults soon grew worse, and one of the locals demanded an apology.

The foreigner became even ruder and louder, and the local chap smashed a beer bottle and took a swipe at his face. Soon, six men were assaulting the Caucasian, kicking and punching him, and no one tried to intervene. I guess they thought he only had himself to blame and secretly hoped he'd learn his lesson.

But his injuries were far more serious than anyone realised. The bashing he'd received had resulted in brain damage. By the time the police arrived to break up the fight, the white man was dead. His assailants had fled, and were never brought to justice.

If it weren't for the blood on the man's face and clothing, I wouldn't have believed his story. And to be honest, Russell, I felt very scared because if his story were true, it meant I was talking to a ghost. In the end, I asked him if he'd come back to Newton Circus seeking revenge on his attackers.

"No," he told me. "I acted shamefully that night and I came back to seek their forgiveness."

ROOM WITH A VIEW

Marion Lee, 39, communications officer

Two years ago, I had to find myself a new home at short notice. My budget was tight and I didn't have the time to be too choosy.

I looked at a few places but they were run-down and I still hoped for something better. Then the agent suggested a place in Jurong West.

It was a fourth-floor walk-up in a pleasant neighbourhood. Light and airy was how the agent had described it and I liked the feel of the place.

As I waited for the agent to arrive, an old lady, who was tending her potted plants on the ground floor, said, "You're not going to live there are you?"

"An agent's going to show me the flat," I said.

She took a deep breath and seemed unhappy. I thought perhaps she didn't like the thought of having me as a neighbour.

I tried to reassure her that I spent my time working not partying.

"I'm not worried about you disturbing me," she said. "I'm worried about what might disturb you."

The auntie's intense manner alarmed me. Was the place full of bats or snakes or something?

I asked her what she meant by that remark.

"The window at the back of the apartment looks straight over Choa Chu Kang cemetery," she told me. "It's the only apartment that does. You have an unobstructed view. Nobody who moves in stays for more than a few days."

"It's okay, Auntie," I said. "I'm not superstitious. I'll look the other way. I'm sure there are plenty of other things to see from that window."

The old lady became agitated. "No, you don't understand," she said. "The spirits sense movement and they are drawn towards it. They're looking for a human body to inhabit so they can escape their graves for a while. They can look directly into that window."

I wasn't sure what to say to that. I was sure the auntie believed it and meant well so I thanked her politely.

At that moment, the agent drove up and I had no intention of walking away without seeing the most promising place that I'd been offered so far. The agent looked flustered and apologised for being late. I assured him that it was fine.

He seemed in a great hurry to leave, almost hustling me up the flights of stairs to the flat.

He must have another client waiting, I thought, one who would offer him a greater gain. Or maybe he just wanted to get home to be with his wife. It was about a quarter to seven. He gave me a very quick tour then returned to wait by the door. I was a little disappointed with his attitude but it didn't make any difference.

The flat was clearly better than anything else I'd seen so far. I made up my mind immediately: I wanted it.

Feeling glad that my search was finally over, I took one last look through the back window. As the auntie had said, the cemetery lay some distance away. It looked peaceful as the sun set and cast a gloomy shadow over the horizon. Nothing to be scared of there.

Then I noticed pin-pricks of light at the cemetery. They seemed to be dancing around the graves. Then they seemed to be moving closer.

I moved closer to the window and peered out. Nothing. It must have been my imagination.

I agreed to take the flat. Shortly afterwards, I moved in. I spent a busy day cleaning and unpacking. Dusk was approaching. Tired but happy, I plodded into the kitchen to make a bowl of instant noodles. As I was filling the kettle, a movement caught my eye.

There seemed to be lights flickering inside the apartment. As I watched in horror, they seemed to move from the hall into the kitchen.

My body went icy cold. Those lights were in pairs. They were eyes!

They advanced into the kitchen and I could make out grey, shadowy bodies around them. There were human shapes in that apartment and they were all looking at me!

One of the creatures moved closer and lifted skeletal hands towards me. There was a mass of rotting black flesh, falling away in parts to reveal the white skull beneath.

I dropped the kettle and screamed. I needed a mirror. That's what my grandmother had told me. A mirror would scare the ghost when it saw its own reflection.

My hands were shaking so much that I could barely unzip my bag. But I managed to tip out the contents and found my powder compact.

It was a small mirror but a mirror nonetheless. With trembling hands, I held it up in the direction of the ghosts.

I shut my eyes tightly. A pounding on the door made me scream once more. They had me surrounded!

There was no way out. In panic, I went to the

window to see if I could somehow climb down.

Then I realised that the lights were receding into the hall. They were backing off. But the hammering on the door persisted. To my relief, it was the old lady checking to see if I was all right.

I collapsed into her arms and started sobbing.

I moved out the next day. I can only wish the next occupants good luck. They'll need it.

HOT IN GEYLANG

Raihan Ibrahim, 26, customer service officer

In *TSGS Book 12,* there was a section on demon possession. I've personally seen it happen.

Although this incident happened about 10 years ago, I still remember it vividly today.

I was working the night shift at a convenience store in Geylang with a friend, Suria. Another colleague, Radiah, who had ended her afternoon shift earlier, stayed on to spend the night with us.

That's what we usually did if we had completed the afternoon shift. We would stay around to "borak-borak" or chit-chat with one another.

As usual, we finished our daily tasks around 2 am and, as there were no customers, we sat outside the store to relax.

As we lit our cigarettes, Suria turned and said, "Han! Look at that tree. Why is it moving?"

I looked at the tree and it did seem to be moving a little.

Radiah didn't pay much attention. She was

tired from a long afternoon.

Suria insisted that we look at that tree. She was getting very worked up.

Suddenly, she threw her cigarette on the floor even though she had only smoked half of it.

"Hey!" I called out. "Why you waste? Cigarettes very precious you know?"

Then I blew smoke in her face for fun.

Suria turned and glared at me. "You know I'm hot?" she said. "You know I'm hot or not?"

Radiah and I were taken aback thinking that she was irritated with me for blowing smoke in her face.

But we were good friends and we frequently teased each other. So I blew smoke in her face again.

She went ballistic. She pointed furiously at my lighted cigarette and shouted, "Fire! Fire! You know I'm hot? I'm very hot!"

Suria's head started to bob up and down and droplets of perspiration ran down her face.

Radiah, being the oldest, tried to calm everyone down. She asked me to recite some prayers in Suria's ear. She said she could not do the prayers as her body was dirty as she had just finished her menses.

I opened my mouth but could not think of anything to say.

Radiah said that she would recite some prayers in her heart and blow it in Suria's ear.

All the while, Suria was howling, "Aku panas! Panas! Panas!" She was complaining of extreme heat. Her face was drenched in sweat, and drops were coming off the tip of her chin.

Radiah kept praying fervently in her heart for about five minutes when Suria suddenly collapsed in a heap.

We dragged her into the store and let her rest till our shift ended.

When she woke up, she said that she had heard somebody whistling after she told us to look at the tree. Then she saw a nenek or old lady walking towards her.

After that, she felt incredibly hot, like she was in an oven.

The strange thing is that even when Suria got up to go home, she couldn't stand up straight. Her body was bent over like an old woman's. We had to support her as she walked.

We quickly called a taxi and sent her home. Her mother immediately sensed that something was very wrong with her daughter.

She told us that a spirit had followed her daugher home. Her mother's spiritual senses were very acute. She told us not to worry and sent us home. We did not see Suria for many weeks.

One day, she came back to work looking like her normal self. She told us that her mother had brought her to the mosque every day for the last 40 days.

Her mother had dutifully offered prayers for her daughter to be cleansed. Suria said that, one day, she finally felt the spirit of the old woman leaving her body.

"It was torture," said Suria. "My mind was totally numb. I hardly remember what happened during that time."

Suria and her mother think that it was the spirit of an old woman, who wanted to feel young again, that had invaded her body.

It was a very traumatic experience for Suria. Even till today, she gets startled every time she hears someone whistling.

GHOST OF BUS 854

Nick Tan, 18, student

It was a cold, wet morning, the kind which is perfect for sleeping in.

But, of course, I had to go to school.

I stumbled onto Bus 854 in Yishun and plonked myself next to a wispy white-haired old lady. She gave me a smile, unusually cheerful for this time of the morning.

I returned her gesture of goodwill and promptly went to sleep, dozing off beside her with music playing in my earphones.

As the bus rumbled on, the passenger crowd started to build up. I was rudely awakened by a few vicious pokes from an umbrella, and opened my eyes to see a middle-aged lady glaring at me.

"Boy, can move in or not? People want to sit down, you know?"

I stared at her, slightly dazed. Turning my head to the left, I saw the old lady peacefully sitting beside me looking out the window, completely unaware of her surroundings.

I looked back at the umbrella-poker with a

curious expression on my face. Couldn't she see the old lady sitting beside me? Was she mad?

The bus was getting packed and commuters were jostling to get in and find a spot to settle in. The middle-aged lady looked puzzled and her eyes flickered to the seat beside me. Her glance passed right through the old woman beside me.

"No one sitting next to you, what... move in leh."

The old lady turned, looked directly into my eyes, and smiled again.

I did not smile back as I was confused. Then the umbrella-poker, losing patience, just made her way past me and plonked herself right on to the old woman's lap.

"Wait!" I screamed. I thought she would crush the old woman's bones.

I turned to my left and saw that only the middle-aged lady was sitting next to me now.

She said brusquely, "I think you have to go to Woodbridge for a check-up."

I looked all around the bus but the old lady had vanished into thin air.

The old lady wasn't scary or anything. In fact, she seemed benevolent and kind.

She just left me feeling rather sheepish as my loud scream made many passengers look curiously in my direction.

I guess I should have stayed in bed after all.

HANDPHONE MESSAGE

Brenda Lee, 12, student

This incident still lingers in my mind.

One Saturday morning, I switched on my handphone and I received a message.

It was from someone I didn't know. The strangest thing was that the sender's phone number had only four digits instead of the usual eight.

The message read, "I'm Teo Gew Chung, a lonely ghost. Send this message to 20 people or I will look you up at 4.44 am to chat with you."

As I wasn't superstitious about such things, I ignored the instructions. In any case, I wasn't going to waste my money forwarding the message to so many people!

I treated it as a joke.

That night, I went to bed at about 3 am after watching television. I was sleeping soundly until I heard someone saying, "Come to me. Come to me."

I opened my eyes and saw a white shadow drifting in front of me. I covered my face with my blanket.

I kept saying lots of prayers. The next morning, I told my mother what had happened.

My mum brought a bomoh to the house. The bomoh told me that it was just a lonely ghost who wanted someone to chat with.

The bomoh managed to "ask" the ghost not to disturb me anymore.

After that, I looked in my phone's Inbox and I

saw that the message had disappeared.

Eerie isn't it, Russell?

Russell Lee: This is the first time I'm hearing that ghosts are using handphones. You must have met a high-tech one, Brenda.

TSUNAMI GHOST

Alan Sit, 52, fisherman

Russell, as you know, the devastating tsunami that struck on December 26, 2004, swept away tens of thousands of innocent people. Because I earn my living from the sea, I can vouch for the fact that their spirits will roam the oceans forever. In fact, I have already had one personal encounter with the ghost of a tsunami victim.

It happened when we went fishing on our boat one stormy night. In a flash of lightning I saw what I thought was a body floating off our starboard bow. It looked nothing more than a bundle of rags with arms and legs but, as men of the sea, we had to do our duty. We immediately cut our engines so we could bring it safely on board.

Russell, I'm sure you are familiar with how human bodies look after they've been immersed in the sea for several days. The facial features become terribly distorted, so much so that not even close relatives can identify the victims. The body itself becomes bloated, and the corpse can look even more gruesome if sharks and fish have been feeding on it. The human eyes are among the first things they devour.

But I will never forget this body as it lay on the deck.

It was a young Indonesian woman, and one of the crew swore she looked like a typical Achenese. Her face was in perfect condition, just as if she was gently sleeping. We saw none of the ravages of the sea, no swelling, no loose skin. Her body was also in normal condition.

Yet we knew she must have been dead for several weeks. It would've taken that long for a body to drift on the currents from the nearest land. We just stood there on the pitching deck, unable to speak. And as I stared at the lovely corpse, I swear I had a vision of her last moments of life. How I received that vision I will never know.

She was living in a seaside village in Aceh when the great waves struck her house. She had been plucked from her bed like so many others and carried out to sea. She had screamed once for her family before the waters claimed her. And then her young life was over.

Maybe it was because her husband had been a fisherman, just like us, that she had "found" our boat in all that wide, empty, storm-tossed sea.

Something told us what she wanted us to do. There was no doubt in our minds that she had "chosen" us to make her last farewells from this life, to ensure her departure was peaceful.

We prayed over her body before returning it to the ocean. It was our privilege to help that beautiful young woman whose soul could now rest in peace.

MY BEST FRIEND

Sandhika Adityadharma, 17, student

Hi, Russell, this is a true story. I experienced it when I was in Secondary One.

My best friend sold his soul to the devil and paid a heavy price for it! He was my classmate in Indonesia. I won't disclose his name because, you know, it's private. I'll call him Pandu.

I'm from Indonesia but I study in Singapore now. Back then, boys in school always tried to impress their girlfriends. I think it's the same in Singapore, right?

My best friend was like that although he looked skinny and ugly (that was his opinion, not mine).

He was always getting beaten up by school bullies.

Pandu took a liking to a girl named Cindy, who was kind of cute, I thought. But she wasn't my type. She was a new student in my school and Pandu couldn't stop thinking about her.

One Saturday, Pandu and I were at the school canteen to buy snacks. There we saw Cindy arguing with a canteen staff. I walked over to help. The canteen staff complained loudly, "She didn't pay me correctly!"

"You lie!" said Cindy. "I paid you! You hid the money, didn't you?!"

That was the day when Pandu and Cindy met. Pandu had come to her rescue, offering to settle the dispute.

"Miss," Pandu said, "this is the money. I pay for her."

When we walked back to our class, Cindy called out to Pandu and said, "Wait! Thanks for helping me. Erm… may I know your name?"

"Me? I am err… nothing."

"Oh, I see," said Cindy, clearly disappointed. "Anyway, once again, thank you for helping me."

"Oh it's nothing, really."

That night, he called me. "Hey, Ninja, do you know that girl? I'm just asking, okay? Don't think I'm…"

He called me Ninja because he thought I looked like a ninja. From his tone, I knew that he liked Cindy.

"Hmm, you like her? He he he, I'll ask her if she likes you."

"Hey! Don't… don't."

He was so shy. I knew him too well.

The next day, he just couldn't concentrate on his lessons because Cindy was sitting beside him.

"What must I do?" he whispered to me.

"Ask her out on a date," I joked.

Soon after, my teacher knocked Pandu's head. "What are you doing?" he asked. "Discussing a love letter for your girlfriend?"

All the students laughed at this. Poor Pandu looked so embarassed.

After class, we went home together with Cindy. She liked to joke and chat with me, not with Pandu. I don't know why.

On our way out of school, we passed two school bullies. They simply stared at us.

"Hey, what a pretty girl!" one of them shouted. "Can we be friends?"

"Leave her alone!" said Pandu.

They were a bit shocked at his brave response. The bully challenged Pandu. "Hey, what are you going to do if I kiss her? You want to fight me? Bring it on…"

And without hesitation, fists flew. Pandu was hit on the head with a stick and he began to bleed. The blood only encouraged them further and they rained blows on his head.

Cindy screamed. It all happened so fast. I managed to smash some of the boys' faces and a couple of them started bleeding too.

They groaned in pain and scooted off. They raised clenched fists and warned, "Wait for our revenge."

They ran away and Cindy calmed down. She looked at Pandu and showed great concern.

She thanked us profusely for helping her when we reached her home.

That night, Pandu called me again.

"Why can't I be strong? Why? I felt so embarrassed that Cindy took care of me when I was supposed to be the strong one. Can you tell me how to be strong, Ninja? You're a ninja, right? You must know how to be strong."

"One day you will be strong," I said. "Just wait. Anyway you're doing fine already."

The next day, I met an all-new Pandu. I mean he was totally different. He cared only for Cindy, and he didn't want to talk to me, his best friend. And during school hours, he would always go to the rest room. I thought it very strange.

One day, I followed him to the washroom because I wanted to know what he was up to.

I saw something that I'll never forget. Are you ready, Russell?

It's really quite disgusting. He had scratched a pentagram sign on his hand with a knife, and the floor was all bloody. He spoke an unknown languge and, to me, it sounded like a spell.

He licked the blood off his hand and prayed loudly, "GIVE ME STRENGTH NOW! LUCIFER!"

I was shocked. What was he doing? I asked him to explain himself.

"You don't understand," Pandu said.

"I think I do."

"You have everything. I have nothing. Cindy likes you. She doesn't even notice me. I prayed to God. He didn't hear me. So I'm praying to the devil."

I tried to stop him and took a towel to clean the blood off his hands.

"San, what do you think you're doing? Get lost, damn it."

I was surprised. He called me "San" and not "Ninja" like he usually did.

I was shocked when he approached me menacingly with his knife. He actually wanted to stab me, his best friend!

Thank God I got away safely. I called the police immediately. And I told the cops, "Get one or two exorcists too! Quickly!"

The police came quickly but without the exorcists because they didn't believe me.

But when they saw Pandu in a trance, a patrol car went out to fetch a well-known exorcist.

The students and teachers had all been asked to leave the school compound because Pandu was prowling around with a knife.

The exorcist, after he had talked to Pandu, shook his head and looked at me sadly, "He has sold his soul to the devil!"

I can't tell you how he exorcised the ghost but after he performed the ritual, Pandu was never himself. He coughed up a lot of blood and died.

But before he died, he asked to meet Cindy.

I rushed out to look for Cindy. When Cindy reached the hospital, he gave her a broad smile. Poor Cindy sobbed uncontrollably. She was fond of him but had been unsure of his feelings for her. The trouble was he was too shy and so could not make himself tell Cindy his true feelings. What a shame!

Pandu died peacefully. He will remain my best friend forever.

He taught me one thing, Russell. And that is not to be jealous of other people's abilities, looks, wealth or talent.

God made everyone different. Be happy being yourself.

Pandu wanted to be strong and brave to impress Cindy at any cost. Instead, he paid the ultimate price.

HANTU RAYA

Evie Tan, 13, student

According to legend, the hantu raya is a ghost that takes the form of a person and impersonates him or her. But it never speaks.

When the hantu raya has been discovered, it will silently walk away and will never be seen again. The following happened at my school in Penang.

David was a lonely boy. This didn't mean that he didn't want to mix with other children. It's just that his classmates didn't like him for some reason. This was the case since kindergarten. He never understood why this was so; he just accepted it.

One day, during recess, David tried to join in with his classmates to play a game. As usual, he was rejected and even teased and insulted. And, as usual, he accepted the rejection and swallowed his anger, frustration and growing hatred.

After school, he was in a somewhat lighter mood and decided to try again. This time, he tried mixing with a group of children playing soccer.

He was not made unwelcome but he was openly left out. No one passed him the ball and some kids kicked him on purpose.

He began to feel really angry and decided to stop playing in case he lost control of himself.

He sat on an empty swing not far from where the children were playing soccer. What he didn't know was that the spot where he was at was the burial place of many Japanese soldiers who had been killed during the Japanese Occupation of Malaysia.

The following day, David appeared in school as usual. Only this time, he did not try to talk to anyone. In fact, he did not talk at all.

His classmates thought that he had finally given up trying.

One classmate, Alex, felt sorry for him and decided to apologise to David for being so mean.

When he didn't get a reply, he tried again, this time actually inviting David to play with him after school.

But all he got for his efforts was a blank stare that revealed no emotion whatsoever.

David didn't seem to care about anything. He seemed to be in a world of his own and nothing in this one meant anything to him.

In the meantime, the teacher walked in and, with a surprised look, said, "David, how can you be here when I just received a phone call from your mother saying that you have a fever and cannot attend school today?"

Still, David remained silent with the same uncaring look on his face. Then he suddenly stood up and walked away.

No one felt like stopping him, not even the teacher.

A week later, David died of a high fever. According to the doctor, the fever was caused by all the anger that had built up in him.

Who, or what, the David look-alike was that day in school will forever remain a mystery.

Was it a hantu raya? We will never know. But David's classmates all feel bad about being mean towards him and wished they had been nicer.

Russell Lee: It's a bit too late to be sorry. Just be more thoughtful from now on.

THE DISAPPEARING DOLLS

Vera Pang, 48, teacher

Russell, I don't usually read ghost stories, but one of my sons suggested I contact you. He said you could answer my question.

Do you have any proof that voodoo is practised here in Singapore?

I know voodoo is very popular in places like Haiti and Africa, but I've never thought it was done here until I saw it myself.

I live in Upper East Coast Road, which is a very modern area full of expensive homes and nice condominiums. Yet recently we experienced voodoo just a block from where we live.

My boys were out walking our dogs one night. It must have been after 10 pm when they came running back to the flat looking terrified. They told me they'd seen some weird dolls on a wall outside a semi-detached house, not too far from the Mobil petrol kiosk. They said the dolls were haunted and had "moved" when they walked past. I told them to stop making up silly stories. Black magic has no place in my home!

That Saturday night, I went to play mahjong

at a neighbour's house. I decided to walk, which meant I had to pass the house my boys had described.

Sure enough, the dolls were sitting on top of a high concrete wall. It was quite dark, and it seemed that the dolls were dressed in rags. As I approached, the dolls began to twist and turn. It was almost as though they were watching me, and making sure I walked past. They had blackened faces, and in the moonlight their expressions looked quite evil.

If the dolls were meant to frighten people away, they were doing a good job!

I ran all the way to my friend's house. She wanted to know why I looked so distressed, but what could I tell her?

After our mahjong game, I was given a lift home. But the next morning when I drove to church I slowed down for another look at the dolls, but they had been removed.

I never saw them again, Russell, and would have forgotten all about the incident, except for the strange events that occurred when the house was being renovated a year later. Dead animals were found buried in shallow graves in the garden, mysterious bloodstains appeared in one of the upper bedrooms, and an old taxi driver swore he'd also seen the dolls on the fence.

There was a lot of rumours going round, Russell. Some said that an Indonesian family had owned the house. They were supposed to be very rich business people with powerful enemies in their own country, and they had a lot of curses put on them.

Others say that an Indonesian girl died in the house and that her toys were seeking revenge. I don't know what to think because I don't believe in voodoo. But then, I also don't believe dolls can move by themselves.

A SPECIAL STORY

Russell Lee: Readers, allow me to introduce the latest member of my team of ghost writers: Becs. She's a student and loves to party.

FEAR OF FLYING

Becs, 16, student

I hate flying. I've always had a fear of heights and being in an oxygen-deprived cabin not only gives me a warping headache, it also wreaks havoc on my usually smooth skin. Couple this with the feeling of claustrophobia that engulfs me the moment I step off the aerobridge onto a plane and well… it's my nightmare. Even the cute flight attendant can't get my mind off my worries — I'm so embarrassed he'll see the sweat dripping from my clammy hands.

But get on a plane I must if I want to see the world and visit my favourite cousin, Victoria, who lives in Houston, Texas. It's my virgin solo flight — at 16, it's about time my parents let me fly unchaperoned. It's so uncool to have to travel with your mum and dad — and I'm glad they finally relented.

Not long after take-off, I feel some movement beside me. I open my eyes slightly and turn down the music from my iPod to hear what's going on. The passenger sitting next to me, a woman clad in a stylish white suit who earlier told me she was from Los Angeles, is speaking to a flight attendant and he looks stressed.

She keeps her voice low but as I strain to hear what she's saying, all I can make out are words like "engine", "problem" and "land".

"You have to ask the pilot to return to Los Angeles. There's a problem with this plane," she says.

"Madam, how would you know that?" the flight attendant questions suspiciously.

"I am not kidding. You have to get the plane back on the ground as soon as possible," she says firmly, but quietly.

What? Could there be an engine problem? Was I going to die? I knew it… it had to happen when I was flying alone. God, you can't take me now, not now, when I haven't said my proper goodbyes to my parents, my pain-in-the butt brother, my best friends at uni… please God, I'm not ready to…

"Don't worry," says Ms LA with her calm voice. "You'll be safe."

I turn to her, my eyes brimming with tears. "Are we going to crash?"

She doesn't say a word but takes my hand in hers.

"Ladies and gentlemen," comes the voice from

the cockpit, "we will be returning to Los Angeles airport for an emergency landing. Please do not panic, stay in your seats and put on your seat-belts. Please cooperate with our crew."

Darn it! I hadn't paid attention to the safety video they had played earlier on — no one does! But now I can't remember what I'm supposed to do in case of an emergency landing!

"Don't worry," the lady in white says. "Just place your hands on the back of your head and bend over during landing. You'll be fine."

It was as if she could read my mind!

I take out my travel journal and begin to write a farewell note:

Dear Mummy and Daddy,

I love you. I know I haven't been the best daughter to you and have hurt you often with my rudeness and, sometimes, uncaring manner. Please forgive me. Please know you mean the world to me, no matter what my mood is or was. Please let James know I love him — even if we fight 24/7.

Becs

Just as I sign off, the pilot says over the inter-com that he will begin the descent. As my ears start to pop, I can see the airport runway from my window seat.

What's actually wrong with the plane? Will we be able to land safely?

When the plane finally touches the ground, it jolts and rattles and comes to a grinding halt after what seems like hours. I am so relieved. Only now do I realise that, all this while, I have my hand in Ms LA's.

"There," she says, "all safe."

It's announced that we'll have to switch planes. While waiting in the transit lounge, I look around for the lady in white to thank her but she's nowhere to be found. I hear two flight staff discussing the problem with the plane. Apparently there was some circuit problem which could have caused grave danger had we continued in the air! *How could that woman have known?*

When we get on the new flight, all passengers are told to return to their previously assigned seats, but I find the one beside mine empty. I tell the flight attendant to make sure the plane doesn't take off without her — this lady who made me feel so safe although she was a total stranger. He walks away to check and returns with a questioning look, "Miss, no one has been assigned this seat."

What? How could that be? There was definitely someone here beside me — I had spoken with her, felt her and touched her. Not only that, she was the one who alerted the flight attendant to the problem — and saved our lives!

As I sit in the plane floating in the clouds, it dawns on me... that woman in white was sent to protect me — my watchful guardian from Los Angeles, the City of Angels.

PART VI

A SPECIAL STORY

THE POKER KING

Wah Bao Yar, 48, unemployed

I read in the newspapers about how Singapore is always on the lookout for a world champion in the sporting arena. Well, Russell, if the card game of poker could be considered a sport, I honestly think that I would have a very good chance.

There are professional tournaments held every year, the biggest being the World Series of Poker which pays the winner a whopping US$7.5 million.

I'm tempted to join but I have decided to keep a low profile. Officially, I'm unemployed but unofficially I have been a card shark for years, playing poker to support myself and my family.

I have done this for close to 30 years now. Some people think of me as a bum but I live in a tastefully furninshed five-room flat and drive a Nissan Cefiro.

Believe me, Russell, I could easily buy a bungalow and drive a top-of-the-line Mercedes if I wanted to. But I don't; simply because I don't want to draw unnecessary attention to myself.

Hundred and even thousands of books have been written about poker strategy. But I have the sure-win method down pat.

For those not familiar with poker, it is a game where you try and make pairs or straights or flushes where all the cards are of the same suit, and the highest combination is the royal flush (10, jack, queen, king, ace of the same suit).

Most of all, a poker player needs luck. Secondly, he needs guts to bluff and to call when he thinks his opponent is bluffing.

It is all a complex game of strategy. But as I said, the key ingredient is luck. Without Lady Luck smiling on you, you cannot win no matter how good you think you are.

So how could I have survived this long as a poker player without getting busted? Well, Russell, the answer is very simple when you think about it.

I have the ability to read minds! In other words, I know what cards my opponents are holding. That makes the game of poker ridiculously simple for me.

It makes it easy to raise the bet when you know your cards are better than theirs and, of course, to fold when they have a better hand.

How can this be possible? It is a secret that I've been keeping to myself for many years. Not even my wife and children know that I have the gift of extra-sensory perception (ESP) or the power to read people's minds.

Scientists have been trying to unlock this mystery for many years but without success. Of course, I'm not going to offer myself up as a guinea pig. It would break my rice bowl.

The term ESP was first coined by Sir Richard Burton in 1870. It was then used by French researcher Dr Paul Joire in 1892. It became popular after the 1920s as researchers and scientists tried to crack this psychic phenomenon.

ESP is often known as the sixth sense after our traditional five senses of sight, touch, smell, taste and hearing.

I don't know why or how I was chosen to be given this sixth sense. I was not born with it.

But when I was eight, I was involved in a car crash. I was in the back seat when a car rammed into the back of my father's vehicle.

The impact sent me flying into the front seat. I suffered superficial injuries but when I woke up in hospital, I couldn't see.

The doctors explained that I had suffered concussion and the impact had caused too much pressure on my optic nerve.

They conducted all kinds of tests on my eyes. One good sign was that I could discern bright light. The doctors were optimistic that I would eventually regain my sight once the pressure on my optic nerve gradually eased.

It seemed an eternity but I was finally able to see again after six months. It was the happiest day of my life and my mother was so overcome with relief that she couldn't stop crying and hugging me.

However, during those six months when my vision was blurred, I had to rely on my other senses. I had no choice.

My ears grew sharper and I could smell the food coming even before the nurse brought it in. It was strange. I couldn't see but I had a heightened awareness of the world around me.

When I finally regained my sight, I vowed

never to take this precious gift for granted again.

I don't know whether it was the knock on my head that jolted my sixth sense. But when I went back to school, I began to hear voices in my head.

I thought I was hallucinating and told my mother so. But she said they would go away.

As the years passed, these voices became clearer and I discovered that they were actually the thoughts of people I came into contact with.

You will be shocked at the degradation and filth which passes through some minds, Russell.

It came to be a way of life and slowly I learned to "tune in" and "tune out" to the thoughts of others.

In the army, I learned various card games like see kee puay, blackjack and chor dai dee. But it was at poker that my ESP gave me the biggest advantage. And poker, traditionally, has been *the* card game with the highest stakes.

I would always look around for poker games, even outside the camp, and I made much more than the pittance which I received from the army.

My parents were alarmed that I was gambling as I never hid the fact from them. "Son, a gambler never has a good end," my mother said.

That advice is true and I've seen many gamblers — whether their vice is horse racing, soccer betting or cards — coming to sorry ends.

"But, Ma, I can't lose. Trust me," I wanted to say. However, I held my tongue as she would have thought I was crazy.

Nevertheless, I moved out after I completed my National Service. I rented a room and looked for poker action all over town.

With my unfair advantage, it was so easy that I got bored easily. There were many occasions that I had to fold a winning hand as I did not want to arouse too much suspicion.

Some nights I won big and other nights I made sure I lost big. But, of course, I made sure I won more than I lost.

Everyone loves a high roller and I got invited to many card games. I made sure not to play with one particular group too often.

One disadvantage of having ESP is that I can hear the other players cursing me when they lose. Many times, I hear profanities being hurled at me in their minds even though they are smiling in my direction. I have built up a steady reserve of funds over the years and I will leave a sizeable bit to charity when I leave this earth.

My three children can look forward to a huge inheritance as well. I pamper my wife with whatever she wants.

Her parents were dead-set against her marrying a gambler but she married me over their objections. I do not play that often anymore as, honestly, it really does get boring when you are guaranteed of winning.

I try to spend quality time with my wife and children instead.

Well, this is my story, Russell. I hope to leave a legacy behind. If you publish my story, I will buy a few copies and leave it for my children so that they will know more about me after I leave this world.

Russell Lee: I enjoyed your story. I will publish it if you agree not to come to my book signings. I am worried that you will read my mind and expose my true identity. Take care, my friend.

A SPECIAL STORY

BISHAN PARK AFTER DARK

Gloria Lee, 21, beautician

On my 18th birthday, I gave myself a huge treat. I let my hair down and partied all night long with my friends, returning home really late. I had an awesome time. I even smoked my first cigarette! I hated it though and almost choked on the smoke. The guys wanted to book into a hotel but I'm not that kind of girl, you know what I mean? What, you don't believe me? Really, puh-leease lah, I have my dignity.

However, when I reached home, Mum shouted at me for returning so late.

She was fuming and suggested that I was living a loose life. And she used other words that hurt me deeply. It was my birthday. Why couldn't she just cut me some slack?

So I went down to Bishan Park to chill out. It was right next to my block of flats.

I was lonely, sad and hurt. I thought of calling somebody but I really couldn't think of anyone. My friends are fair weather friends, you know what I mean? They disappear at the slightest hint of trouble and gather like vultures when there's a good time — or free booze — to be had.

So I was walking alone, deep in thought, when I saw a young man sitting near the huge pond in the park. He was about my age and rather good-looking.

"Hey, bro," I called out, "do you have problems with your folks too?"

He shook his head. I asked him whether I could sit with him. "Cool," he said.

His fine features, long hair and pale skin reminded me of the cute Korean actor Bae Yong Jun. Soon we were talking merrily away like old friends. His name was Alex but I called him Al.

Just when things were warming up, he stood up and said he had to go home. Just like that. I looked at my watch and saw it was 3.55 am.

Since I was still sore, I didn't want to return home just yet. "Let me accompany you," I said.

I asked him where he lived.

"Near the mango tree," was his cryptic reply.

"You mean the mango tree here?" There was a mango tree about 20 metres behind us.

He nodded. "I died here a few months back."

I felt as if my heart would burst. I took a deep breath. "Hey, stop kidding, man," I said, trembling.

Russell, you won't believe this but it's the truth. In front of my very own eyes, he just walked to the mango tree and disappeared!

My knees went weak but I managed to run all the way home. When my mother opened the door, I forgot all the pent-up hostility and told her what had happened. Instead of consoling me, she seemed rather happy! She then rushed to the prayer room and took something in her hand.

"Show me the mango tree," she said.

I thought that she was going to the mango tree to pray for me. But when we got there, she was asking Alex's spirit for a 4D number! Fancy that! I was disappointed, to say the least. Well, that's my mother for you, I guess. All she thinks about is money. I could only slap my forehead in frustration.

But you know what? My mother struck first prize the very next weekend and won $25,000. Talk about lucky.

However, she never bothered to buy anything to thank Alex. I've not stepped foot into Bishan Park since. It's spooky man, you know what I mean?

Russell Lee: There are so many people seeking for supernatural help when it comes to 4D numbers. I wouldn't recommend it though — read the next story.

BRIDE FROM HELL

Lim Seng Ann, 44, businessman

I was a taxi driver for many years, working long hours for about two to three thousand dollars a month.

That money is just about enough to survive in Singapore. Of course, I yearn to have an easier life and have dabbled in Toto and 4D, without luck.

Some friends visit temples and fortune tellers in the hope of getting lucky numbers. Sometimes, I even tag along but instead of getting richer, I find a bigger hole in my pocket from my 4D spending.

A few years ago, a Malaysian girl was brutally murdered by a jealous boyfriend and the story was reported in the papers.

One of my friends suggested that we go to her wake.

"Go for what?" I said. "We don't even know her."

"To get 4D numbers lah, goondu!" my friend Ah Peng said. "You don't know that you can get good numbers from murder victims, meh?"

I really didn't know that but many people apparently read the papers for such cases and attend the wakes for this very reason.

I didn't feel good about it but I went along with Ah Peng. Besides, I didn't want to be goondu.

The dead girl's family was grieving. Even though she wasn't local, there was a sizeable crowd there, including a few reporters.

I followed Ah Peng as he made his way up to the coffin and bowed along with him.

"Please give us a lucky number and we will burn many offerings to you," he said, softly, adding, "thank you."

The next day, we took a bowl and drew some numbers out. They happened to be 4939.

"Remember to bet big," said Ah Peng.

I only had a few thousand dollars' worth of savings in my bank but something told me that my luck might change.

I withdrew $800 and went to a Singapore Pools outlet. I bet 200 big 200 small for the next weekend.

On Saturday, I bought the Chinese evening daily and scanned the 4D results eagerly. But I wasn't even close.

"Oh no! It's all Ah Peng's fault for telling me to bet big. Eight hundred dollars gone down the drain!"

I had been hopeful all week but that old familiar sinking feeling came back. I was driving my taxi as usual on Sunday when I received a call from Ah Peng.

"Brother, ho say liao!! Yoo hoo! We kena first prize, baby!!"

I thought he was joking but he insisted he wasn't. "Just go and buy Wanbao and see for yourself."

I quickly drove over to a 7-11 store and got a copy of the Chinese evening paper. I almost got a heart attack when I saw that 4939 had won first prize that day.

I was a millionaire!

For those who do not play 4D, the payout for my bet was exactly one million dollars.

Ah Peng, a die-hard gambler, had won twice as much as I did. He was in constant trouble with loansharks and lived from day to day.

4D and Toto were his only salvation.

"I owe them so much that I would have had to tiao lao, commit suicide, if this number had not come out."

But within two years, he had blown his money away on womanising and high stakes gambling. He even managed to land himself in debt once again.

The last I heard, he had fled to Thailand to seek refuge. "Easy come, easy go" seems to be a common theme among gamblers.

But anyway, back to my story. I stopped being a taxi driver and started a mini-mart. Business was steady. I was content being a boss and sitting behind the cashier collecting money.

I bought a nice Rolex to complement my towkay image as well.

I burnt a big paper mansion, cars and lots of hell bank notes to the murdered woman and thanked her for her help. But things were not as simple as that.

About a year later, I was driving home after work when a woman, dressed in white, appeared in the passenger seat next to me.

In shock, I swerved the car and almost hit a lamp post.

"Seng Ann, you must pay me back what you owe me," she said. "I am lonely down there. Marry me."

I realised that she was the murder victim. "But I already have a wife here," I said. "How about Ah Peng? You gave him the number as well."

"You are more handsome and I think you are dependable," she said. "Ah Peng is good for nothing and cannot be trusted."

She looked normal except for a deep gash on her neck where she had been slashed.

I was terrified. "Please leave me alone. I will burn more offerings to you," I said.

"You men are all the same," she said, laughing bitterly. "You won a million dollars and you think you have done so much good by burning me a few hundred dollars' worth of offerings.

"What makes you think that I even get them in the first place?

"No! I want you to be with me in hell forever. Did you think about how insensitive you were in going to my funeral to ask for numbers?"

I felt ashamed at her words.

"Hell is a hot place," she continued. "You can save your offerings. Just keep fanning me when you get there in return for your million dollars.

"I will be waiting for you... my future husband!"

She then started laughing and kissed me on the cheek before she left.

I regretted listening to Ah Peng. I had not thought about the consequences although I had known it was simply not right to ask a murdered woman for numbers, with her grieving family nearby at that.

Russell, you have much experience in the supernatural. How can I make things right?

Russell Lee: I can understand why people buy 4D but not the lengths they go to in order to get a winning number. I can only suggest that you look up the murdered girl's family in Malaysia and see if you can help them in some way. Maybe this will appease her anger and bring you some respite.

THE THIEVING TOYOL

K L Chee, 73, retired police inspector

Russell, in my career as a police inspector I encountered many strange cases but none as frightening as this story.

As a police officer I had been trained to deal in the facts and trust only real evidence, not superstition or witchcraft. But when the crime itself used witchcraft, what was I to think?

Twenty-five years ago, there had been many reports of petty theft in the Siglap area. Money had been stolen in coffee shops, small items shoplifted from stores, radios and shopping stolen from unlocked cars.

As usual, we checked through our files of habitual offenders and decided to investigate one particular criminal whom I shall call Zainal. He had a long record of petty crime and had spent much of his life behind the walls of Changi Prison. He had vowed that he would never go back inside.

Zainal lived in an old kampung house in Jalan Tua Kong, right in the heart of Siglap. In those days, there was an old temple there and the kampung around it was the haunt of gangsters and debt collectors. Today, beautiful new houses and condominiums line the winding road.

Zainal's house was almost uninhabitable. The roof had partly caved in, the walls were dilapidated, and thick scrub and overgrown grass made it very difficult to reach the front steps.

When we entered the shadowy house, we immediately heard noises.

It sounded like a child's laughter. We made our way to the big room at the back that served as a kitchen. On the floor were children's toys and, to our amazement, the toys were all moving.

My Malay sergeant stepped back in horror.

"Toyol," he warned me, and led me outside.

We stood in the filthy compound and he explained that the Malay spirits called toyol are little childlike imps who can be trained to steal things.

They look very young, he told me, and love to play games. I must admit I was very sceptical until my sergeant explained how people could go to a bomoh and pay to have a toyol transferred to them for life.

The more I heard, the more I began to wonder if the crafty old Zainal had bought himself a toyol to carry out his criminal work, so that his own hands would be clean of any crime.

But he had made one mistake. Under the house we found a box containing stolen goods including some radios.

A check with our files showed that their serial numbers matched those of the goods reported missing by their owners.

We staked out the house and towards evening Zainal came home. We pounced on him and he was very scared. When we said we were going to arrest him for petty theft, he said he had not done anything wrong.

The court found otherwise and he was gaoled again. When Zainal was being led from the court, he was very agitated. My sergeant explained that if you don't look after your toyol, it could turn on you.

The toyol feeds on blood. Some people always put some food on the table beside their plate for the little devil.

I could understand why Zainal was so alarmed. He would not be at home to look after the toyol. Nor was he able to pay to have the toyol transferred back to the bomoh.

In prison, the wardens became curious. Every morning, Zainal's arms would be covered with bruises. But when he told them his toyol had been pinching him at night, they just laughed.

Early one morning, hideous screams were heard coming from his cell. When the guards got there it was too late. Someone or something had hacked his body to draw blood and he had died in agony of a heart attack.

My sergeant said it was proof that toyols exist. "The child ghost turned on him for his lack of attention and Zainal paid with his life."

A SPECIAL STORY

Russell Lee: Damien Sin filed this final story about his friend, Micky Fu.

A-LI-SHAN DE GU NIANG

Damien Sin, 39, author

My good friend, Micky Fu, met with this encounter. He was in the 3rd Guard Infantry Battalion of the Singapore Armed Forces, stationed in Taiwan.

The harsh life and tough training of the third guardsmen was a bit too harsh and tough for him. And so, he managed to "kheng", malinger, into the position of OC's runner and mess boy. This did not make him popular with the other guardsmen as Micky was fond of strutting about in full crisp uniform and shiny boots, like some dandified mascot.

This did not bother Micky at all. In fact, he was enjoying himself very much as they all headed out to Taiwan.

"A-li-shan de gu niang, mei ru sui ah…"

As the song goes, that was all on Micky's mind: Girls, girls, girls. Especially the girls of Taiwan. He was in love with them all already. He'd been seeing them on TV all his life. They were all beautiful, had manners and were full of wit, grace and charm; not like our local ah huay, ah lian.

But as the 3rd Guard Battalion checked into their fog-bound HQ in the Misty Mountain region, Micky had a surprise in store for him.

The nearest whorehouse was miles and miles away, and so, the soldiers were serviced by a bunch of enterprising ladies who were too old and lazy for farm work. With their toothless grins, they came once a week on bicycles for the "ah bing ge". Because it was a bitterly cold region in a God-forsaken part of the country, the women bathed about once a month and never shaved their legs. But what put Micky off was their armpit hair, it wasn't very romantic at all. And so, he was able to abstain from sin on this occasion. It didn't make him feel very holy, but it made him the laughing stock of the regiment.

And so, Micky kept to himself. In fact, Micky always kept to himself. He did not enjoy the rowdy company of loud-mouthed macho shits. But he did enjoy putting on an aloof air of poetic disdain... although he wasn't much of a poet.

The old fortress that served as battalion HQ for the 3rd Guard was a huge sprawling military complex built by the Kuomintang in the sixties. The architects of Chiang Kai Shek's army had a taste for grandeur, and their lingering loyalties for Imperial China shows in the decadent features of their design.

The parade square was a mini Tiananmen square, and there were pillars and arches that framed the linked compounds just like in the Forbidden City. For the officers' quarters, the higher ranks had landscaped gardens with goldfish ponds and ornate pavilions for afternoon tea ceremonies. Micky liked his surroundings very much. It awakened his sense of imagination. There seemed to be some kind of enchantment just around the corner.

Breakfast in ROC was great. You get hot porridge with anchovies, or yew char kuay and hardboiled eggs. Back home, you only get bread. After breakfast, while the rest of the regiment went out for training, Micky was able to explore all the empty, untenanted spaces of the vast complex.

The 3rd Guard only took up a small section of the big fort. And there was a whole section of the place closed up and cordoned off. This area was supposedly haunted, and it was Micky's favourite part. There was a surreal old children's playground in the little kindergarten compound for the officers' kids. As Micky walked among the creaky swings and rusty roundabouts, he heard a sound coming from within the wishing well, dried up now after years of disuse and neglect.

Micky looked in and saw a baby fox. It had somehow fallen in and hurt its leg.

"Hello! Want to come out, is it?" Micky asked playfully. He laughed as it scrabbled frantically, having seen him. As he looked again, he saw some coins glittering at the bottom of the wishing well.

"Hmm…" he thought, it didn't look too deep. He could get in and out of it easily… but for that fox. Still, it was just a small one. It didn't look like it could hurt him.

"Don't bite me, okay? I'm coming down to help you get out," he said. Micky looked at the strange old dusty coins as the fox snarled suspiciously at him.

"Wei! Bie yaa wo, wo shi lai bang ni ya!" *Hey,*

don't bite me, I'm here to help you! He used Mandarin, in case the fox didn't understand him. This was Taiwan, after all. And the motives of helpful, courteous Singaporeans are so often misunderstood. For though the fox was small, it's tiny little teeth looked razor sharp.

But it was such a cute little thing. Micky felt no fear as he filled the pockets of his Number 4 pants with coins. He was a city boy, quite ignorant about wildlife. After clearing out the silver, he casually picked up the stunned, surprised animal, which squirmed a little on his shoulder as he climbed out again.

It hit the ground running as it got back to the surface, limping a little as it paused for a second to turn around to look at Micky, before running off into the woods.

Micky was in a great mood when he returned to camp. And he spent the rest of the day distracted by his good fortune. OC Major Teo Chee Hong found his runner more distracted and blur than usual when he made his rounds that day.

After inspecting his troops, he went with them on a long winding trek through the dense frost-covered woodlands. They walked in silence for miles. Micky's mind was elsewhere. He couldn't wait to get back to camp and wondered what was going on when Major Teo stopped abruptly in his tracks and whispered, "Psst! Hand me my rifle... quickly."

"Hah? Nah..."

Micky passed the M16, Major Teo was already gesturing with impatience. It was then that he saw the little red fox. It looked liked the one he had saved earlier this morning. Now it stood rooted to the spot, surprised by the human intrusion into this part of the woods. It was only 50 metres away. Major Teo raised the rifle and took aim… and the resounding "click" of misfire echoed through the woods.

"What the heck? Micky, I thought I told you to clean the rifle and keep it well-oiled for me!"

"Sorry, sir."

"Sorry? You can sorry some more?! SAF where got sorry one?"

"But that time the Courtesy Campaign you said…"

"SHADDUP! Go back and report RSM for extra duty."

Micky was silent as he cursed his luck. However, in his heart, he was glad that the fox had got away…

Micky was on "extra" guard duty that very night. But it was not too bad. Quite nice actually. The night was clear and crisp, and the sky up above was ablaze with stars. The moon was so bright, it lit up the surrounding woodlands with a pale luminous glow.

During a break between shifts, Micky walked off alone to smoke a cigarette. As he did, he slipped back into the carefree daydream mode that filled up the days of his National Service.

For Micky was a "happy go lucky" kind of guy.

But a dense pall of darkness fell as the moon was hidden by a vast passing cloud. And then, a swirling icy mist came billowing out of the woods.

As weak moonbeams tore through the wispy fog, Micky saw two figures approach him.

The first flush of fear quickly faded when he saw they were two young peasant girls. They both looked about his age, around 18 or 19, and they were dressed in "tang chuan" traditional costumes, with long silken sleeves and red satin shoes. Micky thought this was strange. But this was Taiwan and it was probably quite normal, he reasoned.

"Ah bing ge", "soldier brother", they addressed him, a common term for SAF soldiers. "Ni tao di shi zhi mo gau te?" "What are you trying to pull?" They teased him with an immediate familiarity.

"Hah? Wo, ah?" "What? Me?" Micky replied.

"Hmm…" they regarded him mysteriously, and talked with each other, ending with a silent nod and smile.

They now spoke to him in a kind of old-style classic Mandarin that Micky only half understood. They seemed to understand his Singaporean-accented Mandarin well enough. They were both so beautiful, Micky couldn't decide which one he liked better. Until the elder of the two introduced herself as "Sakura".

A Japanese name. Micky was sure it wasn't her real name but he liked her better already, since her sister hadn't even bothered introducing herself.

Micky was invited to follow them. They said they were going to a nearby temple, to "ching xiang", to burn joss sticks in offering to mark some coming-of-age ceremony, or some other obscure festival. Micky wasn't sure, but he went along with them anyway.

They took him through a long and winding trail through the woods. The moon was shining now, brighter than before, so that when they came upon a clear crystal lake, its radiance was dazzling on the surface of the gently rippling water.

At the other end of the lake, there was a small waterfall splashing in a curving grotto of ancient moss-covered rocks.

They took his hand and led him across the water, walking on a series of stepping stones that led them straight to a cave behind the sheet of falling water.

The water was freezing as Micky stepped through the waterfall. But as he stood gasping on the other side of it, he saw, within the icy caverns, a massive temple with towering pillars of gold and ivory, before a vast altar hewn from the rock. But the main thing Micky registered about this other-worldly place were the other-worldly "people" there.

For, in Micky's eyes, they were not quite human at all.

Some looked entirely normal, except for a tail hanging from their behind. There were cats' whiskers, rabbit ears, goat horns and fish scales on the animal faces of the men and women there. But Micky's fear was not as great as the terror in their eyes when they saw him.

"It's all right... he's a good mortal. He saved us this morning!" the sisters explained to the rest.

Then, they told the gathered company how Micky pulled one of them from a well, and how a hunter's weapon was "jammed" because of him.

They gathered around him now, with looks of admiration and approval. Micky felt like a hero. Although he couldn't really take credit for his OC's rifle jamming the way it did, he basked in their reverence all the same.

Until a guy, around Micky's own age, stepped forward to denouce him. Micky saw that he, like the sisters, was completely human in form. He also had the same classy elegance. He looked livid as he approached Micky now, snarling slightly, spoiling for a fight.

But the little sister held him at bay, as the elder sister led Micky away, quickly crossing the crystal lake, and back into the woods.

"Thank you for saving me," she said, as she took his hand. They stood together in a clearing where the moon hung low overhead. Micky stared unblinkingly into her face, his heart pounding hard in his chest. And then, with the surreal slow motion of a dream, she closed her eyes and kissed him on the lips.

But the moment was shattered when the hostile guy at the temple burst forth from the bushes with a couple of animal-men; all their eyes shone with the light of hatred for this human Micky.

"Run!"

Micky did as he was told, feeling a soft hand on his back, then a hard shove… and then, he was airborne, running with the wind. The ground vanished under his feet as he raced back to the safety of his camp.

The next few days, a fox was often spotted prowling around the edges of the camp, stalking the soldiers.

"Is she looking for me?" Micky wondered to himself. "Or was it all just a beautiful dream?" If it was a dream, it was a dream he desperately wanted to come true.

Late one Friday evening, as Micky wandered alone in the woods, he was approached by Sakura's younger sister.

"Help, my sister's been caught. They're going to kill her! You must do something before…"

But before she could say another word, Micky was already sprinting back towards the camp.

OC Major Teo was delighted with his prize catch. He planned to send it to the taxidermist in the nearby village to have it snuffed and stuffed. Meanwhile, he planned to keep it in his office overnight.

Being the OC's runner, Micky had the keys to the office, and so he broke in that night and stole the cage. Sneaking it out of the camp, Micky set the fox free.

As it ran into the dense woods, Micky was stunned to see Sakura standing amongst the trees. She stepped forward and picked up the fox in her arms, adding to Micky's confusion.

"Thanks Micky… thanks for your help once again."

"Huh? What's going on here? I thought that was you…"

Sakura let the fox slip out of her arms where

it ran off to safety.

"That was my fiancé," she explained.

Suddenly it all dawned on Micky. He spoke with growing understanding.

"You were only using me all along to make him jealous."

"I'm sorry Micky, but... I'm a fox, and we are like that," she said, shrugging it off with a wistful smile.

Micky felt crushed. "You used me."

"Is it so bad? To be... useful?" she asked, and then she tenderly touched his face, saying, "Don't take it so hard, okay? I'll always remember your kindness... how you helped me, and my sister, too." Then she kissed him long and hard. She was kissing him goodbye.

"Hey, where's your sister now, ah?" Micky said, when he recovered. But she was already gone. And there appeared a pair of MPs led by RSM Warren Tan himself.

"I don't know what you're trying to do. But this time, you've gone too far!" he said, before they clapped him in chains and led him away.

Stealing from the OC's office was a severe disciplinary matter. Although the stolen item wasn't anything official, Micky was to be court martialled.

Sent home in disgrace, he was sentenced to nine months in detention for his conduct.

He told me his story with a smile on his face and a tear in his eye. But he had no remorse, no regrets at all.